smoothies

Healthy Shakes & Blends

smoothies
Healthy Shakes & Blends

Tracy Rutherford

Aurum Press

contents

Recipe list **6**

Introduction **8**

Glossary of fruits **10**

Step-by-step preparing fruits **14**

Selection and storage **18**

DAIRY SMOOTHIES **20**

DAIRY-FREE SMOOTHIES **42**

MILK SHAKES **52**

FRAPPES **66**

DECADENT DRINKS **84**

MOCKTAILS **98**

Glossary of terms **104**

Ingredients index **106**

Health index **110**

Guide to weights and measures **111**

recipe list

DAIRY SMOOTHIES 20

High-fiber smoothie 22

Protein power smoothie 22

Restorative smoothie 22

Cherry–berry smoothie 25

Berry shake 25

Banana and date smoothie 25

Pear, pecan and maple smoothie 26

Pineapple–mint lassi 26

Mango and ginger lassi 26

Strawberry smoothie 29

Favorite banana smoothie 29

Banana–buttermilk blend 29

Apricot and almond smoothie 30

Spiced plum smoothie 30

Blackberry smoothie 30

Fruit and nut smoothie 33

Tropical smoothie 33

Cranberry–vanilla smoothie 33

Spiced pistachio smoothie 34

Breakfast smoothie 34

Smoothie soother 34

Fruit salad smoothie 37

Berry and apple smoothie 37

Summertime blend 37

Peach and mango low-fat smoothie 38

Passion fruit and banana smoothie 38

Fresh fig and ginger smoothie 38

Apricot smoothie 41

Lemon smoothie 41

Pear and flaxseed smoothie 41

DAIRY-FREE SMOOTHIES 42

Orange–peach smoothie 44

Mango oat-milk shake 44

Strawberry–soy thick-shake 44

Cherimoya shake 47

Iced soy latte 47

Muesli mix 47

Pineapple–coconut whip 48

Banana and raisin blend 48

Cantaloupe crush 48

Apricot and passion fruit shake 51

Papaya, lime and coconut smoothie 51

Tahini–date smoothie 51

MILK SHAKES 52

Black currant shake 54

Lemon–passion fruit shake 54

Fruit shake 54

Mocha latte shake 57

Caramel milk shake 57

Chocolate–orange shake 57

Banana split shake 58

Berry yogurt thick-shake 58

Mango milk shake 58

Honey–macadamia shake 61

Chocolate milk shake 61

Caramel–date milk shake 61

Iced coffee shake 62

Orange sherbet shake 62

Vanilla malted milk shake 62

Double chocolate thick-shake 65

Chocolate–caramel thick-shake 65

Peppermint patty shake 65

FRAPPES 66

Minty melon mix 68

Mango, peach and ginger frappe 68

Pineapple, orange and strawberry frappe 68

Papaya, pineapple and mango frappe 71

Papaya, banana and lime frappe 71

Avocado shots 71

Watermelon, strawberry and mint frappe 72

Pink peach frappe 72

Blueberry and banana frappe 72

Mango, pineapple and passion fruit frappe 75

Cranberry, orange and pineapple frappe 75

Vegetable crush 75

Tamarillo, banana and kiwifruit frappe 76

Pineapple–persimmon crush 76

Red papaya and cantaloupe frappe 76

Berry–citrus blend 79

Purple passion 79

Beet, orange and grape blend 79

Carrot and cantaloupe blend 80

Grapefruit and nectarine frappe 80

Raspberry, plum and lime frappe 80

Green tea and melon frappe 83

Watermelon and grape ice 83

Pomegranate and pear ice 83

DECADENT DRINKS 84

Tiramisu shake 86

Blueberry cheesecake shake 86

Apples à la mode 86

Crème caramel shake 89

Black Forest shake 89

Espresso freeze 89

Praline shake 90

Peaches and cream shake 90

Butterscotch–pecan shake 90

Apricot parfait shake 93

Cookies 'n' cream shake 93

Chocolate berry shake 93

Rhubarb smoothie 94

Creamy mandarin shake 94

Warm marshmallow bliss 94

Chocolate–cherry–coconut shake 97

Mango and toasted coconut shake 97

Warm banana–chocolate float 97

MOCKTAILS 98

Banana blitz 100

Strawberry daiquiri 100

Chilled eggnog 100

Coffee thick-shake 103

Spicy Mary 103

Mint tea slush 103

introduction

The term smoothies encompasses various beverages, but in a broad sense it refers to drinks made in a blender. In this book, you will find a chapter offering smoothies based on milk and yogurt and flavored with fresh fruit and other healthful ingredients. A chapter on dairy-free smoothies has recipes that use soy, rice and oat milk, as well as juices, as alternatives to dairy products. These drinks are thickened with soy yogurt, ice cream or sorbet. Other chapters feature traditional milk shakes made with milk and ice cream; frappes, a combination of fresh fruit and ice; dessert-style drinks; and mocktails.

Feel free to modify the recipes to suit your taste and dietary requirements. If you are unable to have dairy products, use dairy-free substitutions. A wide variety of dairy-free ice creams are now available and can be used in recipes that call for traditional ice cream. Conversely, if you like some of the flavor combinations in the chapter of dairy-free drinks, by all means use dairy products instead of the soy or other milk substitutes.

Making these drinks for children is a great way to encourage them to consume valuable nutrients, especially since a frothy smoothie looks like a treat. Be aware, however, that the flavored syrups used in milk shakes are high in sugar. Therefore, these drinks should be saved for special occasions. Drinks flavored with fresh fruit and enriched with yogurt rather than ice cream are the ideal choice for everyday meals and snacks.

Remember as well that young children need a reasonable amount of fat in their diets as an important energy source. Dairy products contain fat along with valuable nutrients and are a much better source of fats than junk foods, which are high in saturated fat but provide no nutrients. For adults and older children, you may replace full-fat products with the low-fat alternatives. If you are not sure when your child can safely move on to low-fat products, check with your pediatrician or a nutritionist.

glossary of fruits

1 Avocado

2 Cantaloupe

3 Cherimoya

4 Fig

1 Avocado

Often thought of as vegetables because of their use in savory dishes, avocados are actually fruits. The skin can be shiny dark green and relatively smooth or purple-black and quite rough, depending on the variety. All have a soft, creamy green flesh around a large round pit.

Avocados are very perishable and should be consumed as soon as they are ripe, which is when they yield to gentle pressure. Unusually for fruit, avocados are relatively high in fat, but the fat is not saturated and has no cholesterol. Avocados are a good source of potassium and beta-carotene. See p 14 for preparation.

2 Cantaloupe

A large round melon with a dull beige skin that has a meshlike texture. The pale orange flesh has a sweet, distinctive musky flavor. They are a good source of beta-carotene and vitamin C. Cantaloupe also has some potassium. Also known as rockmelon.

3 Cherimoya

Also known as custard apple, the cherimoya is a large, vaguely heart-shaped fruit with knobbly, apple green skin and flesh that is a cross between bananas and mangoes in flavor. A ripe cherimoya may have a few dark spots on the skin; more than this, and the fruit is overripe. When ripe, it will give slightly to a gentle squeeze. The cream-colored flesh contains hard black seeds. To prepare a cherimoya, cut in half and scoop out the flesh, discarding the seeds. The seeds can hide in the dense flesh, so make sure you remove them all. Cherimoyas contain vitamin C and some minerals, such as calcium and iron.

4 Fig

The color of figs ranges from very pale green, to red and green, to deep purple-brown, depending on the variety. The flesh ranges from pinkish red to creamy yellow and has many tiny edible seeds. A ripe fig yields to gentle pressure and, because it is highly perishable, should be eaten as soon as possible. Figs are a good source of calcium and potassium, dietary fiber and vitamins A, B and C.

5 Honeydew melon

6 Kiwifruit

7 Mango

8 Papaya

5 Honeydew melon

A large, round to slightly oval melon with smooth, pale green or sometimes yellow skin and pale green flesh. The flavor, though not strong, is sweet and refreshing. Honeydew melons contain some potassium, but no significant amounts of other nutrients.

6 Kiwifruit

The dull, slightly fuzzy skin of the kiwifruit hides a vibrant green interior with a paler core surrounded by tiny edible black seeds. A ripe kiwifruit gives slightly to gentle pressure. If very soft, it is overripe and will have an unpleasant fermented taste. Very rich in vitamin C, kiwifruit also contains vitamin E. See p 16 for preparation.

7 Mango

The mango, with its succulent, voluptuous flesh, is one of the most popular tropical fruits. Color depends on variety; most fruits usually have orange-yellow skin tinged with red. They are ripe when soft to the touch and should be used within a day or two before they become overripe and start to ferment. Avoid mangoes with black patches on the skin, which indicate age. The best sign of a good mango is its pleasantly sweet fragrance. Mangoes are very rich in beta-carotene and vitamin C. See p 14 for preparation.

8 Papaya

A large fruit with silken yellow flesh and yellow skin that may be tinged with green when not quite ripe. The ripe fruit gives easily to gentle pressure; when fully ripe, it bruises easily. To prepare a papaya, cut it in half lengthwise, then scoop out the seeds and discard. Place each half, cut side down, on a cutting board and carefully cut away the skin. Papayas ripen at room temperature. Wrap and refrigerate any unused portion, but only for a short time as the flavor will deteriorate. Papayas are high in beta-carotene and in the enzyme papain, which aids digestion.

9 Passion fruit

10 Persimmon

11 Pineapple

12 Pomegranate

9 Passion fruit

A round fruit with leathery, dark purple skin, which when opened reveals juicy yellow pulp containing many small, black edible seeds. The smooth skin becomes wrinkled over time. If the fruit still feels heavy, it is usable, but very wrinkled fruit may be too old and the pulp inside will be dried out. Passion fruit is a good source of vitamins A and C. See p 15 for preparation.

10 Persimmon

The Hachiya persimmon, the best variety for using in blended drinks, is astringent and unpleasant when underripe but is sweet and juicy when ripe, by which time it is an intense orange-red. Ripe Hachiyas are extremely soft and should be handled with great care to avoid puncturing or bruising. To prepare a persimmon, cut in half and scoop out the pulpy flesh, discarding any seeds. High in vitamin A, these fruits also have calcium, thiamin, potassium and iron.

11 Pineapple

A tropical fruit that resembles a large pinecone, with spiky green leaves protruding from the top. The rough exterior hides juicy, fibrous yellow flesh. It is difficult to select the perfect pineapple, as the appearance gives little away. Generally, make sure the fruit has no soft or bruised areas and that its aroma is sweet and pleasant. Check the bottom to make sure it is not too soft or has mold. Some say that a leaf can be pulled easily from a ripe fruit. If unsure of a pineapple's ripeness, seek the advice of your retailer. Pineapples are a good source of vitamin C and bromelain, an enzyme that aids digestion. Only fresh pineapples contain bromelain, as it is destroyed in the canning process. See p 17 for preparation.

12 Pomegranate

This round fruit has tough, pinkish red skin. Inside there is minimal pulp, along with tough membranes and many seeds. The gorgeous red juice is appreciated for its tart flavor. The seeds are often used as a garnish on sweet and savory dishes. Pomegranates are a good source of vitamin C. See p 17 for preparation.

13 Red papaya

14 Ruby grapefruit

15 Semi-dry dates

16 Tamarillo

13 Red papaya

Similar to the yellow-skinned, yellow-fleshed papaya, but smaller and possessing red-orange flesh. This variety is similarly rich in beta-carotene and also contains the carotenoid lycopene, which is still undergoing study but may be proven to be an even more powerful antioxidant.

14 Ruby grapefruit

Also known as pink grapefruit. This fruit has the same shape as a yellow grapefruit but may be smaller, depending on the variety. The skin has a distinct pink blush, and the flesh is pink-orange. The pink juice is slightly sweeter and not as tart as yellow grapefruit juice. These citrus fruits are high in vitamin C and dietary fiber.

15 Semi-dry dates

These dates have a higher water content than dried dates and are therefore softer in texture. High in natural sugar, the sweet, sticky flesh is very nutritious, containing minerals such as calcium, iron, potassium and magnesium, as well as dietary fiber. Dates have a single pit, which is easy to remove. Dates are occasionally available pitted. See p 16 for preparation.

16 Tamarillo

An oval fruit with a smooth, thick, deep red or yellow-orange skin, depending on the variety. The flesh is orange and contains small edible black seeds. Soft to touch when ripe, tamarillos must be peeled to remove the bitter skin. The flesh has a sharp, tangy flavor that is pleasantly sweet and sour. Tamarillos are a good source of potassium and vitamin A.

preparing fruits

1

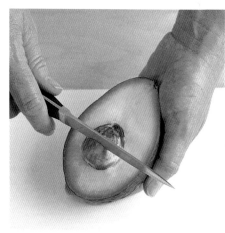

1a

2

2a

This step-by-step guide shows you how to make the most of fruit.

Preparing avocado

1 Cut through the avocado lengthwise and all the way around the pit. Gently twist the halves in opposite directions, then pull apart. The pit will remain in one half.

1a Sharply strike the pit with the blade of a knife, then twist the knife to lift out the pit.

Preparing mango

2 The flat pit runs lengthwise through the fruit, roughly through the center third. Cut the flesh from either side of the pit in one piece, running the knife as close to the pit as possible.

2a Cut each mango piece in half lengthwise, then run the knife between the peel and the flesh to remove as much flesh as possible. Cut any remaining flesh from the pit.

3

3a

4

4a

Preparing passion fruit

3 Pierce the thick skin with the tip of a knife, then slice the fruit in half. Cutting the skin with a sawing motion can be dangerous, as the knife could slip.

3a Scoop the pulp out of the skin with a small spoon.

Peeling fruit

4 To peel soft fruits such as peaches, plums, apricots or tamarillos (pictured), cut a small X in the bottom of each fruit. Place in a heatproof bowl and cover with boiling water. Let stand for about 1 minute. The skin should start to curl away at the X. Drain and rinse under cold running water.

4a When the fruit is cool enough to handle, slip the skin off with your fingers.

5

Peeling kiwifruit

5 Slice the ends off the fruit with a small, sharp knife. Stand the fruit upright and cut off the skin, working your way around the fruit.

6

Pitting dates

6 Cut through each date lengthwise with a small, sharp knife, working the knife around the pit. Pry out the pit with the knife or your fingers.

7

Pitting fruit

7 Cut around the fruit deep enough just to touch the pit with the knife.
7a Gently twist the halves in opposite directions to release them from the pit. Carefully pull out the pit with your fingers or cut out with a small knife.

7a

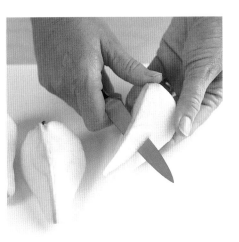

8

9

10

Coring pears
8 Peel the pears, then cut lengthwise into quarters. Cut the core from each quarter.

Coring pineapple
9 Peel the pineapple using the same method shown for kiwifruit. Cut the pineapple lengthwise into quarters, then cut away the core.

Juicing pomegranates
10 Cut the fruit in half crosswise. Use a citrus reamer with a shallow bowl to extract and collect the juice. The goal is to gently crush the membranes and seeds to release the juice. Rather than vigorously twist the pomegranate half, press it against the reamer. Watch out for splashing juice, which will stain fabric. If the juice contains bits of seed or white membrane, pass it through a fine-mesh strainer.

selection and storage

SELECTION

Thanks to modern transportation and refrigeration methods, fruits are now sold year-round in many markets. This is not, however, a guarantee of quality. Fruits sold in your local market but not in season locally have traveled a long distance or have been stored for a long time. As a result, they may lack flavor or not be at their best nutritionally. They are usually more expensive, another reason to avoid them.

For the best taste and nutrition, choose a recipe that uses fruit in season.

The fruit should be ripe and soft enough to blend to a smooth texture. Slightly overripe fruit is suitable, but avoid fruit that is obviously past its prime.

Some fruits, such as bananas, clearly need to be peeled before use. In other cases, such as peaches and plums, removing the skin or peel is a matter of personal taste. The recipes in this book call for peeling such fruits, since the skin can sometimes be a little tough, which affects the texture of the drink.

STORAGE

Whole, uncut fruit should be stored at room temperature in a well-ventilated position, away from direct sunlight. If the fruit is becoming overripe, it may be refrigerated to retard ripening but should be used as soon as possible. Cut fruit should be wrapped in plastic wrap to prevent drying out, then refrigerated, but should also be used as soon as possible.

Berries should be taken from their packaging and picked over for any damaged fruits. If the berries are not being used immediately, do not wash. Place in a single layer on a plate, cover with plastic wrap and refrigerate until required. Use as soon as possible for the best flavor.

Grapes and cherries should be kept in the refrigerator until needed.

FREEZING

Many fruits freeze well for use in drinks. Because some fruits have a fairly short season, freezing them is a great way to extend their season. Time spent preparing and packaging the fruit for freezing is well worth it, especially when the fruit soon disappears from the market or becomes prohibitively expensive.

Once frozen fruit has thawed, its texture is quite soft and mushy, making it unsuitable for recipes requiring fruit with a firm texture and attractive shape. Thawed frozen fruit, however, is excellent for use in blended drinks. To prepare fruit for freezing, peel, pit and chop as called for in a recipe, so no further preparation is needed later apart from thawing. Place in a plastic freezer bag and expel as much air as possible from the bag. Seal securely, label and date. Frozen fruit will keep for two to three months. After this time, the texture may have deteriorated, but the fruit will still be safe to consume.

Fruits suitable for freezing include apricots, bananas, berries, cherries, grapes, mangoes, melons, nectarines, papayas, passion fruit, peaches, persimmons, pineapples and plums.

Package the fruit for frezzing in portions that you will use at one time. Once the fruit is thawed, it should be used immediately.

Berries can first be frozen in a baking pan or on a baking sheet so

1

2

they do not clump together. Then they can be placed in a large lock-top bag and used as needed.

Passion fruit pulp can be scooped into ice cube trays to freeze. The cubes of pulp can then be put into an airtight freezer bag.

PREPARING FRUIT FOR FREEZING

1 Place berries on a baking pan or baking sheet, making sure they are not touching. Place, unwrapped, into the freezer and freeze just until firm. Transfer to lock-top bags or airtight containers, then seal tightly and label.

2 Place peeled, chopped fruit in a freezer bag and spread into a single layer. Expel as much air as possible from the bag, then seal securely.

dairy smoothies

When we were children, our parents encouraged us to drink milk, or consume other dairy products, daily, to obtain the calcium we needed for strong, healthy teeth and bones. Most of the calcium in our bodies is present in our teeth and skeleton, but it is also found in the blood, where it performs such tasks as helping to regulate muscle function, including heartbeat, and normal blood clotting. Blood lacking in calcium will take it from the bones, a calcium storehouse that needs to be replenished daily.

Because maximum bone strength is reached when people are in their early twenties, it is vital that enough calcium has been taken in by that age to establish a solid foundation. Insufficient calcium intake can cause problems later in life, particularly for women, in the form of osteoporosis. It is just as important to maintain calcium intake throughout life, especially when needs are greatest, such as during pregnancy and after menopause.

Milk and other dairy products are sometimes perceived as high in fat, and therefore to be avoided, but low-fat milk is actually higher in calcium than full-fat milk. Although calcium is available in other foods, dairy products are a good source of the mineral because it is readily absorbed by the body. Milk-based smoothies are a delicious way to boost your daily calcium intake. With the addition of fresh fruit and nuts, they become a nutrient-rich treat.

Some recipes in this chapter specify the use of acidophilus yogurt, which contains the bacteria culture *Lactobacillus acidophilus*. This helps to restore the balance of bacteria in the intestines, which can be upset due to illness or taking antibiotics. You may use this specific yogurt whenever yogurt is called for in a recipe.

If you are unable to consume dairy products, you can easily substitute non-dairy milk and yogurt for the dairy products used in this chapter.

High-fiber smoothie

Prunes have laxative qualities and are a good source of iron and potassium. Apples contain pectin, a soluble fiber. The acidophilus yogurt helps to balance the bacteria present in the intestines, making everything work smoothly.

6 pitted prunes, chopped
1 tart apple, peeled, cored and chopped
1/2 cup (4 fl oz/125 ml) water
1 cup (8 fl oz/250 ml) milk
1/2 cup (4 oz/125 g) plain (natural) acidophilus yogurt
1 teaspoon honey
2 teaspoons psyllium husks

In a small saucepan, combine prunes, apple and water. Bring to a boil, reduce heat to low, cover and simmer until very soft, about 10 minutes. The apples will still hold their shape. Set aside to cool. Place prunes, apples and remaining ingredients in a blender and process until smooth and frothy.

Makes about 2 cups
(16 fl oz/500 ml); serves 2

Protein power smoothie

Tofu is a good source of protein and calcium, and also contains some vitamin E. Make sure you buy tofu labeled "silken" for drink recipes; firmer types will not blend to a smooth consistency.

1 cup (8 fl oz/250 ml) milk
4 oz (125 g) silken tofu
1 ripe banana, peeled and chopped
1 tablespoon protein whey powder
1 tablespoon carob powder
2 teaspoons brown sugar or palm sugar

Place all ingredients in a blender and process until smooth and frothy.

Makes about 2 1/2 cups
(20 fl oz/625 ml); serves 2

Restorative smoothie

This thick smoothie is great if you are trying to gain weight or build up your strength after a period of illness. The avocado provides monounsaturated fat, which helps to guard against heart disease. The Brazil nuts are a good source of selenium, an essential trace mineral that promotes normal growth and hormone production.

1 1/2 cups (12 fl oz/375 ml) milk
1/3 cup (3 oz/90 g) plain (natural) yogurt
1 small banana, peeled and chopped
flesh from 1/2 small avocado
5 Brazil nuts
2 teaspoons honey
1/2 teaspoon finely grated lemon zest

Place all ingredients in a blender and process until smooth and frothy.

Makes about 1 1/2 cups
(12 fl oz/375 ml); serves 1

Pictured: Restorative smoothie

Cherry–berry smoothie

Pitting cherries may seem laborious, but using a cherry pitter makes the task quick and easy. Cherries are a good source of potassium and are believed to help in the prevention and treatment of gout, a type of arthritis.

*1/2 cup (2 1/2 oz/75 g) sweet cherries, pitted
1 cup (4 oz/125 g) hulled fresh or thawed frozen strawberries
1 cup (8 fl oz/250 ml) milk
1/2 cup (4 oz/125 g) plain (natural) yogurt
1 teaspoon honey or maple syrup, or to taste*

Place all ingredients in a blender and process until smooth and frothy.

**Makes about 2 1/2 cups
(20 fl oz/625 ml); serves 2**

Berry shake

Frozen yogurt is a tasty alternative to ice cream, and low-fat varieties are available. Regular yogurt can also be used.

*1 cup (4 oz/125 g) hulled fresh or thawed frozen strawberries
1 cup (8 fl oz/250 ml) milk
1 cup (5 oz/150 g) mixed berry frozen yogurt
honey to taste*

Place all ingredients in a blender and process until smooth and frothy.

**Makes about 2 cups
(16 fl oz/500 ml); serves 2**

Banana and date smoothie

For this smoothie, you want to use semi-dry dates, which have a higher moisture content and therefore are softer than dried dates. If only dried dates are available, cook them in *3/4 cup (6 fl oz/180 ml)* water for 10 minutes.

*4 semi-dry dates, pitted and chopped
1/3 cup (3 fl oz/90 ml) water
1 banana, peeled and chopped
1 cup (8 fl oz/250 ml) milk
1/2 cup (4 oz/125 g) plain (natural) yogurt
pinch nutmeg*

In a small saucepan, combine dates and water. Bring to a boil, then reduce heat to low, cover, and simmer until dates are soft, about 3 minutes. Set aside to cool completely. Place dates and remaining ingredients in a blender and process until smooth and frothy.

**Makes about 2 cups
(16 fl oz/500 ml); serves 2**

Pictured: Cherry–berry smoothie

Pear, pecan and maple smoothie

The pears need to be ripe so their flesh is soft enough to blend effectively. When fresh pears are not in season, use about 1 cup (5 oz/150 g) canned unsweetened pears in juice, drained. Toasting the nuts enhances their flavor, but if you use very fresh nuts, they do not need to be toasted.

1/4 cup (1 oz/30 g) pecans
2 ripe pears, peeled, quartered and cored
1 cup (8 fl oz/250 ml) milk
1/2 cup (4 oz/125 g) vanilla yogurt
2 teaspoons maple syrup, or to taste

Preheat oven to 350° (180°C/ gas mark 4). Spread pecans on a baking sheet and bake until fragrant and lightly toasted, about 5 minutes. Set aside to cool, then coarsely chop. Place pecans and remaining ingredients in a blender and blend until smooth and frothy.

Makes about 2 cups
(16 fl oz/500 ml); serves 2

Pineapple–mint lassi

Lassi is a traditional Indian drink made with yogurt, ice, a flavoring such as the mint used here and sometimes, but not always, fruit. Indian drinks and desserts tend to be quite sweet, but this one is not. Adjust the amount of sugar to your taste.

1/2 pineapple, peeled, cored and chopped
1 cup (8 oz/250 g) plain (natural) yogurt
1/2 cup (4 fl oz/125 ml) water, chilled
4 mint leaves
8 ice cubes
2 teaspoons sugar, or to taste

Place all ingredients in a blender and process until smooth. Thin with a little more water if you find the drink too thick.

Makes about 3 cups
(24 fl oz/750 ml); serves 2 or 3

Mango and ginger lassi

This lassi makes a refreshing dessert following a curry or other Indian food. You could also sip it with the meal, as yogurt provides a soothing counterpoint to dishes containing chili peppers. The sweetness of the resulting drink will depend on the sugar content of the fruit.

1 large mango, peeled and flesh cut from pit
1 cup (8 oz/250 g) plain (natural) yogurt
1/2-inch (12-mm) piece fresh ginger, peeled and chopped
1/2 cup (4 fl oz/125 ml) water, chilled
8 ice cubes
2 teaspoons sugar, or to taste

Place all ingredients in a blender and process until smooth. Taste and adjust the sugar to your liking.

Makes about 2¹/₂ cups
(20 fl oz/625 ml); serves 2 or 3

Pictured: Mango and ginger lassi

Strawberry smoothie

If the strawberries lack flavor, use strawberry yogurt, preferably a naturally flavored product, instead of the plain yogurt.

1 cup (4 oz/125 g) hulled fresh or thawed frozen strawberries
1 1/2 cups (12 fl oz/375 ml) milk
1/2 cup (4 oz/125 g) plain (natural) yogurt
honey to taste

Place all ingredients in a blender and process until smooth and frothy.

Makes about 3 cups
(24 fl oz/750 ml); serves 2 or 3

Favorite banana smoothie

If the banana is very ripe, the smoothie may be sweet enough without the honey. Add a couple of teaspoons of wheat germ if you like.

1 large banana, peeled and chopped
1 1/2 cups (12 fl oz/375 ml) milk
1/2 cup (4 oz/125 g) plain (natural) yogurt
honey to taste

Place all ingredients in a blender and process until smooth and frothy.

Makes about 2 1/2 cups
(20 fl oz/625 ml); serves 2

Banana–buttermilk blend

Buttermilk, a low-fat milk product, is cultured, like yogurt, and therefore adds a delicious tang to blended drinks.

1/2 cup (4 fl oz/125 ml) buttermilk
1 cup (8 fl oz/250 ml) milk
1 large banana, peeled and chopped
1 tablespoon honey
pinch nutmeg or cinnamon

Place all ingredients in a blender and process until smooth and frothy.

Makes about 2 cups
(16 fl oz/500 ml); serves 2

Pictured: Strawberry smoothie

Apricot and almond smoothie

Almonds are a good source of vitamin E and although nuts are high in fat, it is mostly unsaturated fat. Dried apricots are a rich source of beta-carotene, which, along with vitamin E, is a valuable antioxidant.

½ cup (3 oz/90 g) dried apricots
¾ cup (6 fl oz/180 ml) water
¼ cup (1 oz/30 g) unblanched raw almonds
1½ cups (12 fl oz/375 ml) milk

In a small saucepan, combine apricots and water. Bring to a boil, reduce heat to low, cover and simmer until the apricots are very soft, about 10 minutes. Set aside to cool. Place apricots and remaining ingredients in a blender and process until smooth and frothy.

**Makes about 2 cups
(16 fl oz/500 ml); serves 2**

Spiced plum smoothie

Use three plums if they are large, or four if they are smaller.

3 or 4 red-fleshed plums, peeled and pitted
1 cup (8 fl oz/250 ml) milk
½ cup (4 oz/125 g) plain (natural) yogurt
honey to taste
pinch ground cinnamon, or to taste
pinch ground cardamom, or to taste

Place all ingredients in a blender and process until smooth and frothy. Taste and add more cinnamon or cardamom if desired.

**Makes about 2 cups
(16 fl oz/500 ml); serves 2**

Blackberry smoothie

Blackberries are often found growing wild in fields or on the side of the road. While it is fun to pick your own berries, they are often considered a weed, so you need to be sure they have not been sprayed with herbicide. Blackberries are a good source of vitamin C and dietary fiber.

1 cup (4 oz/125 g) fresh or thawed frozen blackberries
1 cup (8 fl oz/250 ml) milk
½ cup (4 oz/125 g) plain (natural) or mixed berry yogurt
1 teaspoon finely grated orange zest

Place all ingredients in a blender and process until smooth and frothy.

**Makes about 2 cups
(16 fl oz/500 ml); serves 2**

Variation: Raspberry smoothie. Use raspberries in place of blackberries.

Pictured: Spiced plum smoothie

Fruit and nut smoothie

When choosing yogurt for this drink, look for brands using natural fruit flavoring and no added sugar. Alternatively, use plain (natural) yogurt and add some fresh fruit.

½ cup (3 oz/90 g) golden raisins (sultanas)
2 tablespoons almond butter
1 cup (8 fl oz/250 ml) milk
½ cup (4 oz/125 g) apricot yogurt or other fruit yogurt

Put raisins in a small heatproof bowl and add boiling water to cover. Let stand for 5 minutes, then drain. Place in a blender with remaining ingredients and blend until smooth and frothy.

Makes about 2 cups
(16 fl oz/500 ml); serves 2

Tropical smoothie

This cooling, tangy drink is ideal to prepare on hot days when cooking holds little appeal. Coconut milk is nutritious but is also high in fat, so choose the low-fat product whenever possible.

1 banana, peeled and chopped
¼ pineapple, peeled, cored and chopped
1 mango, peeled and flesh cut from pit
1 cup (8 fl oz/250 ml) low-fat coconut milk, chilled
½ cup (4 oz/125 g) mango or other tropical-fruit yogurt
4 ice cubes

Place all ingredients in a blender and process until smooth and frothy.

Makes about 3 cups
(24 fl oz/750 ml); serves 2 or 3

Pictured: Tropical smoothie

Cranberry–vanilla smoothie

Cranberries contain vitamins C and D, as well as potassium and iron. They are also effective in the treatment of mild urinary-tract infections. The berries are quite tart, so adjust the sweetening to your taste.

1 cup (4 oz/125 g) fresh or thawed frozen cranberries
½ cup (4 oz/125 g) vanilla acidophilus yogurt
1 cup (8 fl oz/250 ml) milk
2 teaspoons honey, or to taste

Place all ingredients in a blender and process until smooth and frothy.

Makes about 2 cups
(16 fl oz/500 ml); serves 2

Spiced pistachio smoothie

The flavors in this drink are reminiscent of Middle Eastern desserts. The fat in pistachios is monounsaturated, and the nuts are a good source of dietary fiber, vitamin B6, thiamin, magnesium and potassium.

1/4 cup (1 oz/30 g) unsalted, shelled pistachios
1 cup (8 fl oz/250 ml) milk
1/2 cup (4 oz/125 g) vanilla yogurt
pinch ground cardamom
pinch ground cinnamon
1 teaspoon superfine (caster) sugar, or to taste
few drops rose water to taste, optional
6 ice cubes

Place all ingredients in a blender and process until smooth and frothy.

Makes about 2 cups
(16 fl oz/500 ml); serves 2

Breakfast smoothie

Another type of fresh fruit in season can be substituted for the apricot. If this smoothie is all you are having for breakfast, make sure not to omit the banana—it is both filling and satisfying.

1 banana, peeled and chopped
2 apricots, peeled and pitted
1 cup (8 fl oz/250 ml) milk
2 teaspoons wheat germ
2 teaspoons oat bran
1/2 cup (4 oz/125 g) plain (natural) acidophilus yogurt
2–3 teaspoons pure maple syrup or honey

Place all ingredients in a blender and process until smooth and frothy.

Makes about 2 cups
(16 fl oz/500 ml); serves 2

Smoothie soother

Pineapple contains the enzyme bromelain, and papaya has the enzyme papain, both of which aid digestion. Acidophilus yogurt helps to restore beneficial intestinal bacteria, and ginger also aids digestion and helps to settle the stomach.

1 cup (8 fl oz/250 ml) fresh pineapple juice
1/2 papaya, peeled, seeded and chopped
1 cup (8 oz/250 g) plain (natural) acidophilus yogurt
1/2-inch (12-mm) piece fresh ginger, peeled and chopped

Place all ingredients in a blender and process until smooth and frothy.

Makes about 2 1/2 cups
(20 fl oz/625 ml); serves 2

Pictured: Smoothie soother

Fruit salad smoothie

Using a frozen banana gives this drink a thick, creamy consistency, but it will be equally delicious with a fresh banana. Bananas are difficult to peel once they are frozen, so peel the banana first, then seal in a plastic bag with the air expelled before placing in the refrigerator. It will take about 3 hours for the banana to freeze.

1/2 cup (2 oz/60 g) hulled fresh or thawed frozen strawberries
1 frozen banana, chopped
2 nectarines, pitted
1/2 cup (4 fl oz/125 ml) fresh orange juice
1/2 cup (4 oz/125 g) vanilla yogurt

Place all ingredients in a blender and process until smooth and frothy.

Makes about 2¹/₂ cups
(20 fl oz/625 ml); serves 2 or 3

Berry and apple smoothie

If you are fortunate to have access to a mulberry tree, then make the most of the short mulberry season by preparing this delicious drink. Other berries in season, such as loganberries or boysenberries, may be substituted.

1 tart apple, peeled, cored and chopped
1 cup (4 oz/125 g) mulberries
1/2 cup (4 oz/125 g) vanilla yogurt
1 cup (8 fl oz/250 ml) milk

Cook apple in a steamer over boiling water until very soft, about 5 minutes. Place apple and remaining ingredients in a blender and process until smooth and frothy.

Makes about 2 cups
(16 fl oz/500 ml); serves 2

Summertime blend

If you are using frozen raspberries, allow them to soften a little but not thaw completely. The cold berries will add a welcome chill to the drink. If you are using fresh raspberries, you may want to add a couple of ice cubes before blending.

2 peaches, peeled and pitted
1 cup (4 oz/125 g) fresh or thawed frozen raspberries
1 cup (8 fl oz/250 ml) milk
1/2 cup (4 oz/125 g) plain (natural) yogurt
2 teaspoons honey, or to taste

Place all ingredients in a blender and process until smooth and frothy.

Makes about 2¹/₂ cups
(20 fl oz/625 ml); serves 2

Pictured: Summertime blend

Peach and mango low-fat smoothie

This drink is so thick and creamy that you might not suspect it is low in fat. It is good to have as a midmorning or afternoon snack to satisfy you until your next meal. If apricot-and-mango yogurt is unavailable, substitute peach-and-mango or mango yogurt.

2 peaches, peeled and pitted
1 cup (8 fl oz/250 ml) low-fat milk
1/2 cup (4 oz/125 g) low-fat apricot and mango yogurt
1/2 cup (3 oz/90 g) fat-free mango sorbet

Place all ingredients in a blender and process until smooth and frothy.

Makes about 3 cups
(24 fl oz/750 ml); serves 2 or 3

Passion fruit and banana smoothie

Passion fruit contain vitamins A and C, as well as dietary fiber. Their sweet, tangy flavor complements banana.

1 banana, peeled and chopped
1 1/2 cups (12 fl oz/375 ml) milk
1/2 cup (4 oz/125 g) vanilla yogurt
2 passion fruit, halved

Place all ingredients, except passion fruit, in a blender and process until smooth and frothy. Scoop pulp from passion fruit and add to blender. Process briefly, until just combined.

Makes about 2 1/2 cups
(20 fl oz/625 ml); serves 2

Fresh fig and ginger smoothie

Figs are a good source of calcium and fiber, and have a high natural-sugar content. Ginger preserved in syrup is used in this recipe. If it is unavailable, substitute a good-sized pinch of ground ginger and sweeten the drink with a little honey.

2 fresh figs, chopped
1/2 cup (4 oz/125 g) vanilla yogurt
1 cup (8 fl oz/250 ml) milk
1 teaspoon chopped preserved ginger

Place all ingredients in a blender and process until smooth and frothy.

Makes about 2 cups
(16 fl oz/500 ml); serves 2

Pictured: Passion fruit and banana
smoothie

Apricot smoothie

Apricots, as with most orange-colored fruits, are a good source of beta-carotene, an antioxidant. Their season is short, so it is good to make the most of fresh apricots.

4 apricots, peeled and pitted
1½ cups (12 fl oz/375 ml) milk
½ cup (4 oz/125 g) plain (natural) yogurt
honey to taste
pinch cardamom, optional

Place all ingredients in a blender and process until smooth and frothy.

Makes about 3 cups
(24 fl oz/750 ml); serves 2 or 3

Lemon smoothie

Lemon zest adds extra lemon flavor to the drink but may be omitted if you like.

1 cup (8 oz/250 g) lemon sorbet
1 cup (8 oz/250 g) vanilla yogurt
½ cup (4 fl oz/125 ml) milk
1 teaspoon finely grated lemon zest, optional

Place all ingredients in a blender and process until smooth and frothy.

Makes about 2 cups
(16 fl oz/500 ml); serves 2

Pear and flaxseed smoothie

Flaxseed, also known as linseed, is a good source of omega-3 fatty acids, which have many health benefits, including the prevention of heart disease. Ground flaxseed and flaxseed oil deteriorate fairly quickly and can become rancid, so this drink is a good way to take advantage of its benefits, as the whole seed is processed in the blender, then the drink is served immediately.

1 cup (8 fl oz/250 ml) low-fat milk
1 cup (8 fl oz/250 ml) low-fat plain (natural) yogurt
honey to taste
1 tablespoon flaxseed
2 pears, peeled, cored and chopped

Place all ingredients in a blender and process until smooth and frothy.

Makes about 2 cups
(16 fl oz/500 ml); serves 2

Pictured: Lemon smoothie

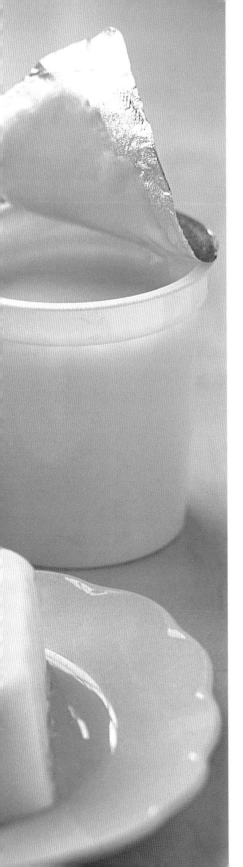

dairy-free smoothies

These dairy-free smoothies and shakes are great for people who cannot tolerate lactose or for vegans who wish to avoid dairy products. The drinks use soy, rice, or oat milk as well as fruit juices as a base and are thickened with soy yogurt, soy ice cream, sorbet and even nuts.

Soy milk is probably the most popular alternative to cow's milk. It is readily available on store shelves in specially sealed packages and also in containers stocked in the refrigerator section alongside regular dairy products. Although soy milk is nutritious, it is best to use milk fortified with calcium if your diet is dairy free. Soy cheeses and margarine-type spreads are also commonly available.

Rice milk and oat milk, other dairy milk substitutes, are made from brown rice and whole-grain oats, respectively. They usually also contain a little oil and water and sometimes salt. These milks are sold in specially sealed containers in some supermarkets and in most health-food stores. Make sure they are well chilled before you use them in these drinks, for the best flavor.

Soy ice creams are often not labeled as such but instead carry a brand name. The recipes here use the generic term to describe any frozen soy ice cream product. Any nondairy frozen dessert could be substituted, such as sorbet, which has the added benefit of usually being fat free. Sorbets are traditionally made from puréed fruit and sugar syrup frozen and churned to a smooth consistency. Other sorbetlike products are on the market. Look for them in the freezer section of your supermarket near the ice cream.

If you are not sensitive to dairy products, you can substitute traditional ice cream or frozen yogurt in any of these drinks.

Orange–peach smoothie

Peaches are easily digestible fruits that contain vitamins A and C, both of which are antioxidants.

1 cup (8 fl oz/250 ml) fresh orange juice
2 peaches, peeled and pitted
1/2 cup (4 oz/125 g) peach soy yogurt

Place all ingredients in a blender and process until smooth and frothy.

Makes about 2½ cups
(20 fl oz/625 ml); serves 2

Mango oat-milk shake

Cashews are a good source of protein and also contain calcium, magnesium and vitamins B1 and B2. They are high in unsaturated fat, which may assist in the prevention of heart disease.

1 cup (8 fl oz/250 ml) oat milk
1 mango, peeled and flesh cut from pit
1/4 cup (1 oz/30 g) raw cashews
1/2 cup (4 oz/125 g) tropical fruit sorbet

Place all ingredients in a blender and process until smooth and frothy.

Makes about 2 cups
(16 fl oz/500 ml); serves 2

Strawberry–soy thick-shake

Silken tofu is the best type to use in drinks, as firmer styles will not blend to a nice smooth texture. Silken tofu is quite fragile and falls apart when handled.

1 cup (8 fl oz/250 ml) soy milk
4 oz (125 g) silken tofu
1 cup (4 oz/125 g) hulled fresh or thawed frozen strawberries
1–2 tablespoons honey

Place all ingredients in a blender and process until smooth and frothy.

Makes about 2 cups
(16 fl oz/500 ml); serves 2

Pictured: Strawberry–soy thick-shake

Cherimoya shake

Cherimoyas, also known as custard apples, have a creamy consistency and a subtle but refreshing flavor. They are a good source of vitamin C and potassium.

1 cherimoya, about 6 oz (180 g)
1 peach, peeled and pitted
1 cup (8 fl oz/250 ml) rice milk
³/₄ cup (6 oz/180 g) vanilla soy ice cream
pinch nutmeg

Cut cherimoya in half and scoop out flesh, discarding the seeds. Place in a blender with remaining ingredients and process until smooth and frothy.

Makes about 2¹/₂ cups
(20 fl oz/625 ml); serves 2

Iced soy latte

For a mocha variation, add 1 tablespoon cocoa powder when dissolving the coffee. You may also need to add a little bit more water.

1 teaspoon instant coffee powder or granules
1 tablespoon boiling water
1¹/₂ cups (12 fl oz/375 ml) soy milk
1 cup (8 oz/250 g) vanilla soy ice cream

In a small bowl, dissolve coffee powder in boiling water and allow to cool. Place in a blender with remaining ingredients and process until frothy.

Makes about 2 cups
(16 fl oz/500 ml); serves 2

Muesli mix

This drink makes a great breakfast when you are on the go. The dried fruits and nuts provide energy and fiber, and wheat germ is a good source of vitamin E and B vitamins.

¹/₄ cup (1¹/₂ oz/45 g) dried apricots
¹/₄ cup (³/₄ oz/25 g) dried apples
³/₄ cup (6 fl oz/180 ml) water
1 cup (8 fl oz/250 ml) oat milk
¹/₄ cup (1¹/₂ oz/45 g) unblanched raw almonds
¹/₂ cup (4 oz/125 g) vanilla soy yogurt
2 teaspoons wheat germ

In a small saucepan, combine apricots, apples and water. Bring to a boil, reduce heat to low, cover and simmer until fruit is very soft, about 10 minutes. Set aside to cool. Place fruit and remaining ingredients in a blender and process until smooth and frothy.

Makes about 2 cups
(16 fl oz/500 ml); serves 2

Pictured: Iced soy latte

47

Pineapple–coconut whip

Pineapples are very refreshing fruits that are a good source of vitamin C and fiber. They also contain the enzyme bromelain, which works to break down proteins, making it a digestive aid. Only fresh pineapples contain bromelain, as it is destroyed in the process of canning.

1/4 pineapple, peeled, cored and chopped
1 cup (8 oz/250 g) tropical fruit sorbet
1 banana, peeled and chopped
1 1/2 tablespoons unsweetened shredded dried (desiccated) coconut
8 ice cubes

Place all ingredients in a blender and process until smooth and frothy.

Makes about 2 cups
(16 fl oz/500 ml); serves 2

Banana and raisin blend

Macadamias are high in calories and fat, but the fat is monounsaturated, which is believed to reduce levels of blood cholesterol. They are also a good source of protein and potassium.

1/3 cup (2 oz/60 g) golden raisins (sultanas)
1 1/2 cups (12 fl oz/375 ml) rice milk
1 banana, peeled and chopped
1/3 cup (1 1/2 oz/45 g) raw macadamia nuts

Place raisins in a small bowl and add boiling water to cover. Let stand for 5 minutes, then drain. Place raisins and remaining ingredients in a blender and process until smooth and frothy.

Makes about 2 cups
(16 fl oz/500 ml); serves 2

Cantaloupe crush

You may also freeze the cantaloupe well in advance of preparing the crush, then thaw it partially before using. The texture of the semi-frozen fruit gives the drink a thick, icy consistency.

1/4 cantaloupe (rockmelon), peeled, seeded and chopped
1 cup (8 oz/250 g) vanilla soy yogurt
1/2 cup (4 fl oz/125 ml) fresh orange juice

Place cantaloupe cubes in a freezer bag, seal and freeze until partially frozen, about 1 hour. Place cantaloupe and remaining ingredients in a blender and process until smooth and frothy.

Makes about 2 cups
(16 fl oz/500 ml); serves 2

Pictured: Cantaloupe crush

Apricot and passion fruit shake

Making this quantity of juice from fresh apricots requires a lot of fruit, so use commercially prepared juice that does not have added sugar or preservatives. Passion fruit are a good source of vitamin C.

2 passion fruit, halved
1½ cups (12 fl oz/375 ml) apricot nectar
1 cup (8 oz/250 g) vanilla soy ice cream

Scoop passion fruit pulp into a blender. Add remaining ingredients and blend until smooth.

Makes about 2 cups
(16 fl oz/500 ml); serves 2

Papaya, lime and coconut smoothie

If desired, you can sweeten this drink with a little honey, brown sugar or palm sugar. The amount you add will depend on the sweetness of the papaya. The tartness of lime offsets the sometimes cloying flavor of papaya.

1 cup (8 fl oz/250 ml) low-fat coconut milk
½ papaya, peeled, seeded and chopped
½ lime, peeled and seeded
8 ice cubes

Place all ingredients in a blender and process until smooth and frothy.

Makes about 2 cups
(16 fl oz/500 ml); serves 2

Pictured: Papaya, lime and coconut smoothie

Tahini–date smoothie

Tahini, used in Middle Eastern dishes such as hummus, is a paste made from ground sesame seeds. It is rich in calcium and unsaturated fat. If you have dried dates, rather than semi-dry, cook them in ¾ cup (6 fl oz/ 180 ml) of water for 10 minutes.

4 semi-dry dates
⅓ cup (3 fl oz/90 ml) water
1 cup (8 fl oz/250 ml) soy milk
1 tablespoon tahini
pinch cinnamon

In a small saucepan, combine dates and water. Bring to a boil, reduce heat to low, cover and simmer until dates are soft, about 3 minutes. Set aside to cool. Place dates and remaining ingredients in a blender and process until smooth and frothy.

Makes about 1½ cups
(12 fl oz/375 ml); serves 1 or 2

milk shakes

Certain foods and beverages are evocative pleasures. Just hearing the word milk shakes can bring to mind one's childhood days of such simple delights as long summer vacations and days at the beach—and enjoying a shake with family and friends. While a glass of milk may be an enjoyable part of the daily diet, the addition of a big scoop of ice cream and some flavoring or fruit, whipped into a frothy confection, becomes a real treat.

The milk shakes in this chapter range from old-fashioned favorites to contemporary and healthful innovations. Some are flavored with syrups available from most supermarkets and could be varied with the addition of fruit to increase the nutrient content. In place of full-fat ice cream, you can use low-fat ice cream, frozen yogurt or even sorbet, which is largely fat free. This way, you can enjoy these drinks without too much guilt.

Milk shakes are fun to make with children. Offer them a chance to come up with their own flavor combinations. Along the way, you can promote the inclusion of fresh fruit and seize an opportunity to slip in a brief lesson about nutrition while giving them a special treat.

Black currant shake

Black currants are one of the richest sources of vitamin C, and drinks made from the syrup can be a healthy alternative to soft drinks. Be aware, however, that these syrups are high in sugar and should be well diluted. This drink makes an interesting change for kids and the milk provides the added benefit of calcium.

1 cup (8 fl oz/250 ml) milk
1 cup (8 oz/250 g) vanilla ice cream
3 teaspoons black currant syrup
1 teaspoon finely grated orange zest, optional

Place all ingredients in a blender and process briefly until frothy.

Makes about 2¹/₂ cups
(20 fl oz/625 ml); serves 2 or 3

Lemon–passion fruit shake

The fragrance of passion fruit is unsurpassed, and the flavor is both sweet and tangy. These fruits are a good source of vitamins A and C.

2 passion fruit, halved
1 cup (8 fl oz/250 ml) milk
1 cup (8 oz/250 g) lemon sorbet

Scoop passion fruit pulp into a blender and add milk and sorbet. Process until combined and frothy.

Makes about 2 cups
(16 fl oz/500 ml); serves 2

Fruit shake

Offering this shake is a great way to entice anyone who doesn't regularly eat fresh fruit to do so. Bananas and strawberries are a good combination for the taste buds of fussy eaters. Other soft fresh fruits in season, such as peaches or other berry varieties, may be substituted.

1¹/₂ cups (12 fl oz/375 ml) milk
1 banana, peeled and chopped
¹/₂ cup (2 oz/60 g) hulled fresh or thawed frozen strawberries
¹/₂ cup (4 oz/125 g) vanilla ice cream

Place all ingredients in a blender and process until smooth and frothy.

Makes about 2¹/₂ cups
(20 fl oz/625 ml); serves 2

Picture: Lemon–passion fruit shake

Mocha latte shake

Coffee and chocolate, known as mocha, is a delicious flavor combination. This is a drink for adults, as children should not consume caffeine.

1 teaspoon instant coffee powder or granules
1 tablespoon boiling water
1½ cups (12 fl oz/375 ml) milk
1 cup (8 oz/250 g) vanilla or chocolate ice cream
1 tablespoon chocolate syrup
sweetened cocoa powder for serving

In a small bowl, dissolve coffee powder in boiling water. Allow to cool, then combine with milk, ice cream and syrup in a blender and blend briefly until frothy. Pour into glasses and dust with cocoa.

Makes about 2½ cups (20 fl oz/625 ml); serves 2

Caramel milk shake

Look for a good-quality caramel syrup. It can also be used as a sauce on ice cream, fruit and other desserts. You can add a banana to this drink, which not only increases its nutritional value but makes it absolutely delicious.

1½ cups (12 fl oz/375 ml) milk
1 cup (8 oz/250 g) vanilla ice cream
2 tablespoons caramel syrup

Place all ingredients in a blender and process until frothy.

Makes about 2½ cups (20 fl oz/625 ml); serves 2

Chocolate–orange shake

Orange sorbet may be used in place of the ice cream and orange zest. The zest adds to the intensity of the orange flavor, however, so you can still include it if you like.

1½ cups (12 fl oz/375 ml) milk
1 cup (8 oz/250 g) vanilla ice cream
1 tablespoon chocolate syrup
1 teaspoon finely grated orange zest

Place all ingredients in a blender and process briefly until frothy.

Makes about 2½ cups (20 fl oz/625 ml); serves 2

Picture: Mocha latte shake

Banana split shake

This drink has all the flavors of a banana split blended together and served in a glass. Choose a peanut butter without added salt or sugar.

1½ cups (12 fl oz/375 ml) milk
1 tablespoon natural peanut butter
1 cup (8 oz/250 g) vanilla ice cream
1 tablespoon chocolate syrup
1 banana, peeled and chopped

Place all ingredients in a blender and process until smooth and frothy.

Makes about 2½ cups
(20 fl oz/625 ml); serves 2

Berry yogurt thick-shake

You can use only one type of berry, if you like, or use a combination of different types.

1 cup (8 fl oz/250 ml) milk
1 cup (8 oz/250 g) mixed berry yogurt
1 cup (8 oz/250 g) vanilla ice cream
1 cup (2 oz/60 g) fresh or thawed
frozen blueberries, or
1 cup (2 oz/60 g) fresh or thawed
frozen raspberries, or
½ cup of each

Place all ingredients in a blender and process until smooth and frothy.

Makes about 3 cups
(24 fl oz/750 ml); serves 2 or 3

Mango milk shake

Sorbet is virtually fat free. If you make this shake with low-fat milk, it is quite a healthy drink—with the bonus of beta-carotene and vitamin C from the mango.

1½ cups (12 fl oz/375 ml) milk
1 mango, peeled and flesh cut from pit, then chopped
½ cup (4 oz/125 g) tropical fruit sorbet

Place all ingredients in a blender and process until frothy.

Makes about 2½ cups
(20 fl oz/625 ml); serves 2

Picture: Berry yoghurt thick-shake with raspberries

Honey–macadamia shake

Toasting the macadamia nuts is advisable as it seems to accentuate their flavor. Like most nuts, macadamias are a good source of unsaturated fat, which helps to reduce blood cholesterol.

1/2 cup (2 1/2 oz/75 g) macadamia nuts
1 1/2 cups (12 fl oz/375 ml) milk
1 cup (8 oz/250 g) vanilla ice cream
1 tablespoon honey

Preheat oven to 350°F (180°C/ gas mark 4). Spread nuts on a baking sheet and bake until fragrant and lightly toasted, about 5 minutes. Let cool, then coarsely chop. Place nuts and remaining ingredients in a blender and process until smooth and frothy.

Makes about 2 1/2 cups
(20 fl oz/625 ml); serves 2 or 3

Chocolate milk shake

Choose a high-quality brand of ice cream that will give the shake a creamy rather than icy texture. You could use chocolate ice cream to intensify the flavor if you like.

1 1/2 cups (12 fl oz/375 ml) milk
1 cup (8 oz/250 g) vanilla ice cream
2 tablespoons chocolate syrup
1 oz (30 g) milk chocolate, optional

Place all ingredients except milk chocolate in a blender and process until frothy. If you like, finely grate chocolate and sprinkle on top.

Makes about 2 1/2 cups
(20 fl oz/625 ml); serves 2

Caramel–date milk shake

This drink is very sweet from the natural sugars in the dates as well as the caramel syrup. The flavor combination is divine, but you may like to tone it down by adding a little more milk, according to your taste.

4 semi-dry dates, pitted and chopped
1/3 cup (3 fl oz/90 ml) water
1 1/2 cups (12 fl oz/375 ml) milk
1 cup (8 oz/250 g) vanilla ice cream
1 tablespoon caramel syrup
pinch ground nutmeg
pinch ground cinnamon

In a small saucepan, combine dates and water. Bring to a boil, reduce heat to low, cover and simmer until dates are soft, about 3 minutes. Set aside to cool. Place dates and their liquid with remaining ingredients in a blender and process until smooth and frothy.

Makes about 2 1/2 cups
(20 fl oz/625 ml); serves 2

Picture: Chocolate milk shake

milk shakes

Iced coffee shake

For this drink, brew your own coffee, as the intense coffee flavor is essential. True coffee aficionados will grind their own beans, but as long as you begin with good purchased ground coffee, prepared correctly, that will suffice.

2 cups (16 fl oz/500 ml) freshly brewed coffee, chilled
2 cups (16 oz/500 g) vanilla ice cream
pinch cinnamon
sugar to taste

Place coffee, ice cream and cinnamon in a blender and process briefly until frothy. Taste and add sugar, if desired.

Makes about 2¹/₂ cups
(20 fl oz/625 ml); serves 2

Orange sherbet shake

Orange may seem like an unusual flavor for a milk shake, but it is delicious. The zest contains oils that carry the intensely aromatic orange flavor.

2 teaspoons finely grated orange zest
1 cup (8 fl oz/250 ml) orange juice, chilled
¹/₂ cup (4 fl oz/125 ml) milk
1 cup (8 oz/250 g) vanilla ice cream

Place all ingredients in a blender and process until frothy.

Makes about 2¹/₂ cups
(20 fl oz/625 ml); serves 2 or 3

Vanilla malted milk shake

This shake is a classic. Malt is derived from barley and is sold as either liquid malt or malted milk powder. The liquid is a thick brown syrup that contains phosphorus and magnesium, and the powder is dried malt combined with dried milk. Both are fortifying, nutritious products.

1¹/₂ cups (12 fl oz/375 ml) milk
1 cup (8 oz/250 g) vanilla ice cream
dash vanilla extract
1 tablespoon malted milk powder or liquid malt

Place all ingredients in a blender and process until frothy.

Makes about 2¹/₂ cups
(20 fl oz/625 ml); serves 2

Picture: Orange sherbet shake

Double chocolate thick-shake

This drink is for chocoholics. It is not everyday fare—but everyone deserves a treat once in a while.

1 cup (8 fl oz/250 ml) milk
2 cups (16 oz/500 g) chocolate ice cream
2 tablespoons chocolate syrup
1 oz (30 g) milk chocolate, optional

Place all ingredients except milk chocolate in a blender and process until frothy. Pour into glasses. If you like, finely grate chocolate and sprinkle on top.

Makes about 3 cups
(24 fl oz/750 ml); serves 2

Chocolate–caramel thick-shake

Chocolate and caramel is a combination made in heaven. You could use vanilla ice cream and add chocolate syrup along with the caramel, if that is what you have on hand.

1 cup (8 fl oz/250 ml) milk
2 cups (16 oz/500 g) chocolate ice cream
2 tablespoons caramel syrup

Place all ingredients in a blender and process until frothy.

Makes about 2 cups
(16 fl oz/500 ml); serves 2

Peppermint patty shake

Rather than hard peppermint candies, use the soft patties coated with chocolate. The green food coloring is not essential, but you can add it just for a bit of fun.

1½ cups (12 fl oz/375 ml) milk
1 cup (8 oz/250 g) vanilla ice cream
2 soft, chocolate-covered peppermint candies, chopped
green food coloring, optional

Place all ingredients in a blender and process until smooth and frothy.

Makes about 2½ cups
(20 fl oz/625 ml); serves 2

Picture: Peppermint patty shake

frappes

A frappe (pronounced frap-ay) is made by crushing ice to a smooth consistency with fruit and other flavorings. Frappes are a great way to consume fruit in a drink since all the flesh is used, as opposed to juices, which leave the fiber behind.

You will need to be sure that your blender is capable of processing ice cubes. Most new models have a speed you can set for ice and by processing in short bursts, the ice is pulverized to a smooth texture. If your blender is not powerful enough to crush ice, you can wrap the ice cubes in a clean kitchen towel and hit them firmly with a rolling pin or mallet to break them into smaller pieces, then process them in the blender.

The recipes in this chapter call for ice by the number of cubes and assume the use of a standard tray of fourteen compartments, each with a capacity of 3 teaspoons. If your trays make larger or smaller cubes, just estimate how much ice you need.

The proportions in the frappe recipes are fairly elastic, so don't worry about getting the amounts absolutely exact.

You can use fresh, canned or frozen fruit, but remember that one of the joys of fresh fruit drinks is using produce in season, when it is at its freshest and tastiest and is most economical. You can make the most of fruits that have a limited season by freezing them for later use (pages 18–19).

If you use frozen fruits, allow them to thaw partially—so the juices are released—to help the blender function properly. The more frozen the fruit, the thicker the drink will be, and you may need to add some water to thin it. You may also reduce the number of ice cubes, to avoid diluting the flavor too much. For the best results, wait until the fruit is thawed and soft. Where juice is called for, it is best to use fresh juice. Citrus fruits are easy to juice, but if you don't have a juicer for other types of fruits, choose the best quality, most natural product you can find.

Minty melon mix

If you have a juicer, make your own apple juice; alternatively, use a natural commercial juice. Pour the juice into ice cube trays and freeze until solid. If not using the cubes immediately, remove them from the trays and store in an airtight lock-top plastic bag to preserve their flavor. The cubes will keep well for a couple of months in the freezer and are handy to have on hand. The mint adds a flavor lift to this drink, so include it if fresh mint leaves are available.

1/4 honeydew melon, peeled, seeded and chopped
2 kiwifruit, peeled and chopped
8 apple juice ice cubes
3 fresh mint leaves, optional

Place all ingredients in a blender and process until smooth.

Makes about 2 cups
(16 fl oz/500 ml); serves 2

Mango, peach and ginger frappe

Mangoes and peaches are good sources of beta-carotene, a valuable antioxidant. Ginger aids digestion and helps to alleviate nausea. Consider taking it before a trip if you suffer from motion sickness. It is also a safe way to treat morning sickness during pregnancy.

1/2-inch (12-mm) piece fresh ginger, peeled and chopped
1 large mango, peeled and flesh cut from pit
2 peaches, peeled and pitted
8 ice cubes

Place all ingredients in a blender and process until smooth.

Makes about 2 cups
(16 fl oz/500 ml); serves 2

Pineapple, orange and strawberry frappe

Frozen fruit can be used while still partially frozen, but it is a good idea to allow it to soften a bit, which makes it easier to blend. Frozen fruit makes the drink quite thick. You may need to add a little water.

1/4 pineapple, peeled, cored and chopped
1 cup (4 oz/125 g) hulled fresh or thawed frozen strawberries
1 large orange, peeled, seeded and chopped
8 ice cubes

Place all ingredients in a blender and process until smooth.

Makes about 2 1/2 cups
(20 fl oz/625 ml); serves 2

Picture: Minty melon mix

Papaya, pineapple and mango frappe

The addition of fresh basil may seem unusual, but it adds an interesting flavor note. Basil is said to boost the immune system.

1/4 papaya, peeled, seeded and chopped
1/4 pineapple, peeled, cored and chopped
1 mango, peeled and flesh cut from pit
8 ice cubes
4 fresh basil leaves, optional

Place all ingredients in a blender and process until smooth.

Makes about 2 cups
(16 fl oz/500 ml); serves 2

Papaya, banana and lime frappe

Bananas add a creamy thickness to blender drinks. One of the most widely consumed fruits, bananas are a good source of potassium, which balances the effect of a high sodium intake and helps to regulate the heart muscle.

1/2 papaya, peeled, seeded and chopped
1 banana, peeled and chopped
1/2 lime, peeled and seeded
6 ice cubes

Place all ingredients in a blender and process until smooth.

Makes about 1 1/2 cups
(12 fl oz/375 ml); serves 1

Avocado shots

In this amazingly fresh-tasting drink, cucumber, lemon and cilantro offset the creaminess of the avocado. Poured into small glasses, it is served as an aperitif. The frappe has a thick consistency. You could thin it with a little water if you like, but don't dilute too much.

flesh from 1 small avocado
1 lemon, peeled and seeded
1 large cucumber, peeled, seeded and chopped
1/3 cup (1/3 oz/10 g) fresh cilantro (fresh coriander) leaves
10 ice cubes

Place all ingredients in a blender and process until smooth. You may need to stop the blender, scrape down the sides of the container with a rubber spatula, then blend again.

Makes about 1 cup
(8 fl oz/250 ml); serves 4

Picture: Avocado shots

71

Watermelon, strawberry and mint frappe

This is a very cooling summer drink. The mint not only adds a refreshing note but also aids digestion, making this frappe a welcome finish to a substantial meal.

1¹/₂ cups (9 oz/280 g) chopped and seeded watermelon
1 cup (4 oz/125 g) hulled fresh or thawed frozen strawberries
6 fresh mint leaves
8 ice cubes

Place all ingredients in a blender and process until smooth.

Makes about 2 cups
(16 fl oz/500 ml); serves 2

Pink peach frappe

Fragrant fruits combine to make an ideal summertime drink. Red-fleshed plums are higher in beta-carotene than those with yellow flesh, but you can use whatever is available.

1 cup (4 oz/125 g) hulled fresh or thawed frozen strawberries
2 peaches, peeled and pitted
2 red-fleshed plums, peeled and pitted
8 ice cubes

Place all ingredients in a blender and process until smooth.

Makes about 2 cups
(16 fl oz/500 ml); serves 2

Blueberry and banana frappe

To freeze a banana, peel first, then seal in a plastic bag with the air expelled before placing in the freezer. It will take about 3 hours for the banana to freeze. Frozen banana gives this drink such a creamy consistency that you would think it contains ice cream.

1 frozen large banana, chopped
2 oranges, peeled, seeded and chopped
1 cup (4 oz/125 g) fresh or thawed frozen blueberries

Place all ingredients in a blender and process until smooth.

Makes about 2 cups
(16 fl oz/500 ml); serves 2

Picture: Watermelon, strawberry and mint frappe

Mango, pineapple and passion fruit frappe

This drink has a beautifully thick, icy consistency. If you find it too thick, thin with a little water or orange juice.

2 passion fruit, halved
1 mango, peeled and flesh cut from pit
1/2 pineapple, peeled, cored and chopped
8 ice cubes

Scoop out passion fruit flesh and place in a blender. Add remaining ingredients and blend until smooth.

Makes about 1 1/2 cups
(12 fl oz/375 ml); serves 2

Cranberry, orange and pineapple frappe

When peeling the orange, leave on some of the white pith, which contains bioflavonoids, which are antibacterial and antiviral. Cranberry juice and pineapple are good sources of vitamin C.

1 orange, peeled, seeded and chopped
1/4 pineapple, peeled, cored and chopped
1 cup (8 fl oz/250 ml) cranberry juice
8 ice cubes

Place all ingredients in a blender and process until smooth.

Makes about 2 cups
(16 fl oz/500 ml); serves 2

Vegetable crush

Red bell pepper is a good source of beta-carotene and vitamin C, and tomatoes contain the carotenoid lycopene, which may help to prevent prostate cancer. Garlic has powerful antibacterial and antiviral qualities. Celery is a good source of potassium and is a diuretic. You may like to season this drink with a little salt and pepper, or just pepper.

1 large red bell pepper (capsicum), seeded and chopped
1 large tomato, cored and chopped
2 stalks celery, trimmed and chopped
1 small clove garlic, peeled
6 ice cubes
6 fresh basil leaves
salt and pepper, optional

Place all ingredients except salt and pepper in a blender and process until smooth. Taste, add salt and pepper if desired, and blend again.

Makes about 2 cups
(16 fl oz/500 ml); serves 2

Picture: Vegetable crush

Tamarillo, banana and kiwifruit frappe

Tangy tamarillos marry well with kiwifruit. They are a good source of vitamin C, as is the kiwifruit, and of potassium, as is the banana. Choose the red-skinned variety of tamarillo rather than the yellow for a prettier colored drink.

2 tamarillos, peeled and chopped
1 banana, peeled and chopped
2 kiwifruit, peeled and chopped
8 ice cubes

Place all ingredients in a blender and process until smooth.

Makes about 1¹/₂ cups
(12 fl oz/375 ml); serves 1 or 2

Pineapple–persimmon crush

Truly ripe Hachiya persimmons are very soft, so soft they seem almost overripe, but this is when they taste the best. Persimmons are a good source of vitamin C, beta-carotene and potassium.

2 ripe Hachiya persimmons
¹/₄ pineapple, peeled, cored and chopped
8 ice cubes

Cut each persimmon in half and scoop out flesh; discard seeds. Place in a blender with remaining ingredients and blend until smooth.

Makes about 1¹/₂ cups
(12 fl oz/375 ml); serves 1

Red papaya and cantaloupe frappe

Red papaya and cantaloupe are both sources of beta-carotene. Red papaya also has lycopene, another antioxidant.

¹/₂ red papaya, peeled, seeded and chopped
¹/₄ cantaloupe (rockmelon), peeled, seeded and chopped
¹/₄ small lemon, peeled and seeded
6 ice cubes

Place all ingredients in a blender and process until smooth.

Makes about 1¹/₂ cups
(12 fl oz/375 ml); serves 1

Picture: Red papaya and canteloupe frappe

Berry–citrus blend

Berries and citrus complement one another beautifully. In addition, this drink is a powerfully nutritious blend of antioxidants in the form of bioflavonoids and vitamins. Antioxidants are believed to help in the prevention of disease and to slow physical degeneration.

½ cup (2 oz/60 g) fresh or thawed frozen blueberries
½ cup (2 oz/60 g) fresh or thawed frozen raspberries
½ cup (2 oz/60 g) hulled fresh or thawed frozen strawberries
2 large oranges, peeled, seeded and chopped
8 ice cubes

Place all ingredients in a blender and process until smooth.

Makes about 2 cups
(16 fl oz/500 ml); serves 2

Purple passion

The purple comes from the blueberries, which contain flavonoids that promote healthy eyesight. They also help to strengthen arteries and veins.

2 passion fruit, halved
¼ pineapple, peeled, cored and chopped
½ cup (2 oz/60 g) fresh or thawed frozen blueberries
8 ice cubes

Scoop out passion fruit flesh and place in a blender. Add remaining ingredients and process until smooth.

Makes about 2 cups
(16 fl oz/500 ml); serves 2

Beet, orange and grape blend

Bottled beet juice is available in most supermarkets. You can also make your own juice in a juicer, using three medium beets to yield the amount required. Beets are a good source of folic acid, iron and calcium. The vitamin C in the orange helps the body to absorb iron. The grapes contribute antioxidants and potassium.

½ cup (4 fl oz/125 ml) beet (beetroot) juice
1 orange peeled, seeded and chopped
1 cup (4 oz/125 g) seedless red grapes
8 ice cubes

Place all ingredients in a blender and process until smooth.

Makes about 2 cups
(16 fl oz/500 ml); serves 2

Picture: Berry–citrus blend

Carrot and cantaloupe blend

This drink is high in the antioxidants beta-carotene and vitamin C. It is best to make your own fresh carrot juice if you have a juicer.

1/2 cup (4 fl oz/125 ml) carrot juice
1/4 cantaloupe (rockmelon), peeled, seeded and chopped
1 large orange, peeled, seeded and chopped
6 ice cubes

Place all ingredients in a blender and process until smooth.

Makes about 2 cups
(16 fl oz/500 ml); serves 2

Grapefruit and nectarine frappe

Ruby grapefruit is not quite as tart as yellow grapefruit. It is rich in vitamin C and dietary fiber.

1 ruby grapefruit, peeled, seeded and chopped
2 nectarines, pitted
6 ice cubes

Place all ingredients in a blender and process until smooth.

Makes about 2 1/2 cups
(20 fl oz/625 ml); serves 2

Raspberry, plum and lime frappe

Red-fleshed plums are high in antioxidants that cleanse the body of damaging free radicals. The tiny seeds in raspberries can be removed by pureeing the berries, then passing them through a fine-mesh sieve, before placing in the blender.

1 cup (4 oz/125 g) fresh or thawed frozen raspberries
2 plums, peeled and pitted
1/2 lime, peeled and seeded
6 ice cubes

Place all ingredients in a blender and process until smooth.

Makes about 2 cups
(16 fl oz/500 ml); serves 2

Picture: Carrot and cantaloupe blend

Green tea and melon frappe

Green tea is said to be a rich source of antioxidants. Make a strong pot of your favorite green tea, let cool, then pour into ice cube trays to freeze. This drink is very simple but utterly refreshing on a hot day.

14 green tea ice cubes
1/4 honeydew melon, peeled, seeded and chopped

Allow cubes to soften slightly. Place cubes and melon in a blender and process until smooth.

Makes about 2 cups
(16 fl oz/500 ml); serves 2

Watermelon and grape ice

Any variety of nondairy frozen sorbet may be used in place of the strawberry.

1 cup (6 oz/180 g) seedless red grapes
1 1/2 cups (9 oz/280 g) chopped and seeded watermelon
1 cup (8 oz/250 g) strawberry sorbet

Place all ingredients in a blender and process until smooth.

Makes about 2 1/2 cups
(20 fl oz/625 ml); serves 2

Pomegranate and pear ice

Prepare the pear juice ice cubes as for the apple juice ice cubes on page 68. This ice also makes a delicious palate cleanser between courses. The recipe can easily be increased.

1 pomegranate
14 pear juice ice cubes
1 teaspoon finely grated orange zest

Cut pomegranate in half crosswise. Use a citrus reamer with a bowl to extract juice (see page 17). Set aside. Place pear juice ice cubes and orange zest in a blender and pulse to blend mixture to a grainy consistency. Divide between 2 small chilled glasses and drizzle with pomegranate juice. Serve immediately, accompanied with small spoons.

Makes about 1 cup
(8 fl oz/250 ml); serves 2

Picture: Watermelon and grape ice

decadent drinks

This chapter veers away from super-healthy drinks and heads into more decadent territory. Some of the flavor combinations are inspired by classic desserts. In fact, these drinks could be called "dessert in a glass." They are a treat served after a dinner party or as an indulgent snack. The beauty of these beverages is that they are quick and easy to prepare, and the flavors are deliciously faithful to their more conventional counterparts. These are the drinks to make when you want to splurge.

Of course, the end product is only as good as what goes into it, so choose the best quality ingredients. Some of the recipes call for rich ingredients, but you can reduce the fat content by using low-fat dairy products. You could also substitute soy milk or other dairy-free alternatives for the milk, and use soy ice cream or frozen yogurt in place of ice cream. If you are serving for a number of guests, the recipes may be doubled or tripled. You will have to make these larger quantities in batches, to avoid overfilling the blender.

Some recipes call for spices measured by the pinch, literally the amount you can pick up between forefinger and thumb tip, or on the end of a pointed knife. Some spices are not as strong as others, so you can afford to aim for a larger pinch, but if you are unsure, start with just a tiny bit, taste, then add more if you like.

Tiramisu shake

Mascarpone, an ingredient in the Italian dessert tiramisu, is an Italian fresh cheese with a thick, creamy consistency and a slightly tangy flavor. This drink is delicious with ladyfingers, another component of the Italian dessert. Feel free to dunk them in the drink.

1 cup (8 fl oz/250 ml) milk
½ cup (4 oz/125 g) mascarpone
3 teaspoons superfine (caster) sugar
2 tablespoons cold strong black coffee
sweetened cocoa for serving

Place all ingredients except cocoa in a blender and process until frothy. Pour into serving glasses and dust with cocoa.

Makes about 2 cups
(16 fl oz/500 ml); serves 2

Blueberry cheesecake shake

The flavors of classic blueberry cheesecake are faithfully reproduced in this drink. Even without using low-fat milk, the shake is still lower in fat than a slice of cheesecake.

1 cup (8 fl oz/250 ml) milk
3 oz (90 g) soft cream cheese
1 cup (4 oz/125 g) fresh or thawed frozen blueberries
1 teaspoon confectioners' (icing) sugar
1 teaspoon finely grated lemon zest
few drops vanilla extract

Place all ingredients in a blender and process until smooth and frothy.

Makes about 2 cups
(16 fl oz/500 ml); serves 2

Apples à la mode

This drink has all the appeal of a good apple pie and none of the bother of making pastry.

2 tart apples, peeled, cored and chopped
1 cup (8 fl oz/250 ml) milk
½ cup (4 oz/125 g) vanilla ice cream
1 teaspoon brown sugar
pinch cinnamon

Cook apples in a steamer set over boiling water until very soft, about 5 minutes. Set aside to cool. Place apples and remaining ingredients in a blender and blend until smooth and frothy.

Makes about 2 cups
(16 fl oz/500 ml); serves 2

Picture: Blueberry cheesecake shake

Crème caramel shake

Look for prepared custard in cartons in the refrigerator section of your supermarket. Reduced-fat varieties are available, and because of the thick consistency, you can barely tell the difference.

1 cup (8 fl oz/250 ml) chilled vanilla custard
½ cup (4 fl oz/125 ml) milk
1 cup (8 oz/250 g) vanilla ice cream
2 teaspoons caramel syrup, or to taste

Place all ingredients in a blender and process until smooth and frothy.

Makes about 2½ cups
(20 fl oz/625 ml); serves 2 or 3

Black Forest shake

The inspiration for this drink is the famous Black Forest cake, a delicious chocolate cake with a Morello cherry filling. Morello cherries are sometimes called tart, or sour, cherries. They are not edible raw but, bottled in syrup, have a distinctive tang. Make sure that the cherries are all pitted before you blend them.

1½ cups (12 fl oz/375 ml) milk
1 cup (8 oz/250 g) chocolate ice cream
½ cup (3 oz/90 g) drained bottled Morello cherries
1 tablespoon chocolate syrup

Place all ingredients in a blender and process until smooth and frothy.

Makes about 2½ cups
(20 fl oz/625 ml); serves 2

Espresso freeze

For this drink, you will need a blender that can process ice cubes. Use a good quality coffee and serve the drink in little glasses after dinner. The recipe may be doubled to serve four without overloading the blender.

1 cup (8 fl oz/250 ml) strong black coffee
2 tablespoons sweetened condensed milk
pinch cinnamon
few drops vanilla extract

Let coffee cool, then pour into ice cube trays and freeze until solid. Place cubes in a blender and pulse in short bursts until grainy. Add remaining ingredients and process until combined. Spoon into small chilled glasses and serve immediately, accompanied with small spoons.

Makes about 1 cup
(8 fl oz/250 ml); serves 2

Picture: Espresso freeze

Praline shake

*¹/₂ cup (³/₄ oz/20 g) sliced
(flaked) almonds
¹/₂ cup (2 oz/60 g) superfine
(caster) sugar
1 tablespoon water
1 cup (8 fl oz/250 ml) milk
1 cup (8 oz/250 g) vanilla ice cream*

Line a baking sheet with aluminum foil
and brush lightly with oil. Place
almonds on foil close together in a
single layer. Combine sugar and water
in a small saucepan over medium
heat and cook until sugar is dissolved
and syrup turns golden brown, about
5 minutes. Take care that mixture
does not burn. Carefully pour syrup
over almonds to coat and let cool.
When praline is cold and hard, after
about 5 minutes, break into pieces,
place in a food processor and
process until finely ground. Place half
of ground praline in a blender with
milk and ice cream, and blend until
smooth and frothy.

**Makes about 2 cups
(16 fl oz/500 ml); serves 2**

Peaches and cream shake

This shake demands perfectly ripe
fresh peaches. It can also be made
with canned peaches when not in
season. Use fruits packed in natural
juice rather than heavy syrup.

*2 peaches, peeled and pitted, or
4 canned peach halves
¹/₂ cup (4 fl oz/125 ml) natural peach
juice or ¹/₂ cup (4 fl oz/125 ml) juice
from canned peaches
¹/₂ cup (4 fl oz/125 ml) milk
1 cup (8 oz/250 g) vanilla ice cream
pinch ground cinnamon or ground
nutmeg, or both*

Place all ingredients in a blender and
process until smooth and frothy.

**Makes about 2¹/₂ cups
(20 fl oz/625 ml); serves 2**

Butterscotch–pecan shake

It is worth the effort to make your own
butterscotch sauce. In a pinch, you
could use a commercial sauce;
choose a good quality brand for the
best flavor.

*1 tablespoon butter
2 tablespoons heavy (double) cream
1 tablespoon brown sugar
few drops vanilla extract
¹/₄ cup (1 oz/30 g) pecans
1 cup (8 fl oz/250 ml) milk
1 cup (8 oz/250 g) vanilla ice cream*

Place butter, cream and sugar in a
small saucepan over low heat and stir
until butter has melted, sugar has
dissolved and mixture is smooth. Stir
in vanilla, pour into a small bowl and
let cool. Place butterscotch mixture
and remaining ingredients in a blender
and process until smooth
and frothy.

**Makes about 2 cups
(16 fl oz/500 ml); serves 2**

Picture: Peaches and cream shake

Apricot parfait shake

Amaretti are Italian almond-flavored cookies with a very crisp, dry texture that lends itself to absorbing liquids, by being dunked in coffee or used in parfaits. Here they thicken a drink that also contains apricots. Peaches may be substituted. Look for prepared custard in cartons in the refrigerator section of your supermarket.

6 amaretti (about 1¹/₂ oz/45 g)
4 canned apricot halves
1 cup (8 fl oz/250 ml) chilled vanilla custard
¹/₂ cup (4 fl oz/125 ml) milk

Place amaretti in a plastic bag. Twist open end and hold it firmly, then break up cookies with a mallet or rolling pin. Place amaretti with remaining ingredients in a blender and process until smooth and frothy.

**Makes about 2 cups
(16 fl oz/500 ml); serves 2**

Cookies 'n' cream shake

This drink is delicious made with chocolate cookies sandwiching a vanilla filling, but you can also use other types of cookies.

6 chocolate sandwich cookies, each 1¹/₂–2 inches (4–5 cm) in diameter
1¹/₂ cups (12 fl oz/375 ml) milk
¹/₂ cup (4 oz/125 g) vanilla ice cream

Place cookies in a plastic bag. Twist open end and hold it firmly, then break up cookies with a mallet or rolling pin. Place cookies with remaining ingredients in a blender and process until smooth and frothy.

**Makes about 2 cups
(16 fl oz/500 ml); serves 2**

Chocolate berry shake

Dark chocolate is superb in this drink, but milk chocolate or white chocolate may be substituted. Already roasted hazelnuts may be purchased. To roast raw hazelnuts, follow instruction for roasting pecans in Pear, Pecan and Maple Smoothie, page 26.

2 oz (60 g) dark chocolate, finely grated
1 cup (4 oz/125 g) fresh or thawed frozen raspberries
1 cup (8 fl oz/250) milk
1 cup (8 oz/250 g) chocolate ice cream
¹/₂ cup (1 oz/30 g) chopped roasted hazelnuts (filberts)

Place all ingredients in a blender and process until frothy.

**Makes about 2¹/₂ cups
(20 fl oz/625 ml); serves 2**

Picture: Cookies 'n' cream shake

Rhubarb smoothie

Rhubarb is very tart and requires sugar to make it palatable. Once sweetened, it has a delicious piquant flavor. Rhubarb contains calcium, potassium and thiamin. Make sure you discard the rhubarb leaves, which are toxic.

2 stalks rhubarb, trimmed and cut into
1-inch (2.5-cm) pieces
2 tablespoons water
1 tablespoon brown sugar
1-inch (2.5-cm) piece cinnamon stick
1 cup (8 fl oz/250 ml) orange juice
1/2 cup (4 oz/125 g) vanilla yogurt

In a saucepan, combine rhubarb, water, sugar and cinnamon stick. Cover and cook over low heat, stirring occasionally, until rhubarb is very soft and pulpy, about 10 minutes. Set aside to cool completely, then discard cinnamon stick. Place rhubarb in a blender with orange juice and yogurt and process until smooth.

Makes about 2¹/₂ cups
(20 fl oz/625 ml); serves 2

Creamy mandarin shake

Star anise has a mild anise flavor, whereas cardamom has an intense, slightly citruslike fragrance. Rosewater, used in Middle Eastern desserts, has a lovely sweet perfume. Any of these additions enhance this drink, but it is also good without them.

3 mandarin oranges, peeled, seeded and chopped
1 cup (8 oz/250 g) vanilla ice cream
1 cup (8 fl oz/250 ml) milk
pinch ground star anise or ground cardamom, or a few drops rose water, optional

Place all ingredients in a blender and process until smooth and frothy.

Makes about 2¹/₂ cups
(20 fl oz/625 ml); serves 2

Warm marshmallow bliss

This drink can also be made with dark chocolate, but the white chocolate has a distinctive flavor that marries well with marshmallows.

1¹/₂ cups (12 fl oz/375 ml) milk
3 oz (90 g) white chocolate, chopped
1/2 cup (1 oz/30 g) coarsely chopped white marshmallows
sweetened cocoa powder

Place milk in a small saucepan over medium heat and heat until hot but not boiling. Remove from heat, add chocolate and marshmallows and stir until they begin to soften and dissolve. Warm blender container by filling it with hot water, then emptying it. Pour milk mixture into blender and process until smooth and frothy. Pour into thick glasses or mugs, and dust with cocoa.

Makes about 2 cups
(16 fl oz/500 ml); serves 2

Picture: Warm marshmallow bliss

Chocolate–cherry –coconut shake

Fresh cherries have a short season, so you can use frozen or canned cherries if necessary. Grate the chocolate on the finest rasps of a grater.

2 oz (60 g) dark chocolate, finely grated
1 cup (8 fl oz/250 ml) low-fat coconut milk
1 cup (8 oz/150 g) vanilla ice cream
1/2 cup (2 1/2 oz/75 g) fresh, frozen or drained canned sweet cherries, pitted
1 oz (30 g) dark chocolate, finely grated, for serving (optional)

Place all ingredients, except dark chocolate for serving, in a blender and process until frothy. If you like, sprinkle finely grated dark chocolate on top.

Makes about 2 cups
(16 fl oz/500 ml); serves 2

Mango and toasted coconut shake

This thick, creamy drink makes a cool treat on a hot summer day.

2 tablespoons unsweetened shredded dried (desiccated) coconut
2 mangoes, peeled and flesh cut from pit
1 cup (8 oz/250 g) mango sorbet
1 cup (8 oz/250 g) vanilla ice cream
1/2 cup (4 fl oz/125 ml) milk

Place coconut in a dry frying pan and toast over medium heat, stirring constantly, until golden. Transfer to a plate to cool. Place in a blender with remaining ingredients and blend until smooth and frothy.

Makes about 2 1/2 cups
(20 fl oz/625 ml); serves 2 or 3

Warm banana–chocolate float

This delicious drink is worth the effort.

2 bananas
3 oz (90 g) milk chocolate, broken into pieces
1 1/2 cups (12 fl oz/375 ml) milk
2 scoops vanilla ice cream

Preheat oven to 350°F (180°C/ gas mark 4). Peel bananas and cut in half lengthwise. Place on a sheet of aluminum foil and arrange chocolate pieces on top. Mold foil around bananas so chocolate remains on top and crimp foil to make a parcel. Place on a baking sheet and bake for 15 minutes. Meanwhile, heat milk in a saucepan over medium heat until hot but not boiling. Remove parcel from oven, carefully unwrap and place bananas and melted chocolate in blender. Add heated milk and process until frothy. Divide between heatproof glasses or mugs and top each with a scoop of ice cream.

Makes about 2 1/2 cups
(20 fl oz/625 ml); serves 2

Picture: Chocolate–cherry–coconut shake

mocktails

The blender is a terrific piece of equipment for whipping up cocktail-type drinks. In fact, such cocktails date back to the 1930s, after the invention of a blender capable of crushing ice. Although daiquiris and margaritas are often considered frozen drinks, both started as simple preparations mixed in a cocktail shaker, and they are still often served that way. Some of the recipes in this chapter are based on well-known cocktails and drinks, reworked to become new favorites.

Mint Tea Slush is a combination of the mint julep and iced tea. Both these drinks are very refreshing on a hot summer day, and especially so when combined. Feel free to experiment. Here, for instance, you may want to use a favorite herbal tea, or you may try substituting lemon verbena or pineapple sage in place of the mint, if you grow herbs in your garden. Other drinks, such as the Coffee Thick-Shake and the Chilled

Eggnog, are not frozen drinks as such but are creamy variations on familiar themes.

Using frozen fruit juice, rather than juice with the addition of ice cubes, gives the drinks a fuller flavor and counteracts the diluting influence of the ice. As for all smoothies, use good quality ingredients.

All the drinks here are great to offer guests as a non-alcoholic alternative at a dinner party, cocktail party or casual get-together, or just to have at the end of a long day to unwind. If you want to serve large numbers of people, make the drinks in batches so you don't overload the blender.

Banana blitz

Reminiscent of a piña colada, this drink is thickened with banana and has a lovely pineapple flavor. To make the pineapple ice cubes, pour pineapple juice into ice cube trays and freeze until solid. If you don't have time to make the ice cubes, double the juice and use ice cubes made with water.

1 large banana, chopped
8 pineapple juice ice cubes
1/2 cup (4 fl oz/125 ml) pineapple juice
1/2 cup (4 fl oz/125 ml) low-fat coconut milk

Place all ingredients in a blender and process until smooth.

Makes about 2 cups
(16 fl oz/500 ml); serves 2

Strawberry daiquiri

It is best to make this drink when strawberries are at the peak of their season and are sweet, ripe and juicy. Use frozen strawberries if you know they are good quality.

2 cups (8 oz/250 g) hulled fresh or thawed frozen strawberries
12 ice cubes

Place all ingredients in a blender and process until smooth.

Makes about 2 cups
(16 fl oz/500 ml); serves 2

Chilled eggnog

Eggnog doesn't always have to be warm, as this tasty drink proves. If you are serving this drink for a special occasion, make your own custard using a vanilla bean. Otherwise, use prepared custard, sold in cartons in the refrigerator section of supermarkets.

1 cup (8 fl oz/250 ml) chilled vanilla custard
1/2 cup (4 fl oz/125 ml) milk
1 cup (8 oz/250 g) vanilla ice cream
ground nutmeg for serving

Place custard, milk and ice cream in a blender and process until smooth. Divide among glasses and dust with nutmeg.

Makes about 2 cups
(16 fl oz/500 ml); serves 2

Picture: Strawberry daiquiri

Coffee thick-shake

Experiment with different flavors of brewed coffee for this one.

1 cup (8 fl oz/250 ml) milk
2 cups (16 oz/500 g) chocolate ice cream
3 tablespoons brewed coffee
pinch ground cinnamon, optional
sweetened cocoa for serving

Place all ingredients except cocoa in a blender and process until frothy. Pour into glasses and dust with cocoa.

Makes about 3 cups
(24 fl oz/750 ml); serves 2 or 3

Spicy Mary

This drink is great to make in summer when tomatoes are at their peak. Serve before dinner with some appropriate hors d'oeuvres.

1 lb (500 g) ripe tomatoes
1/2 lemon, seeded and chopped
1 teaspoon Worcestershire sauce
few drops Tabasco, or to taste
4 ice cubes
salt and freshly ground black pepper, to taste

Place all ingredients except salt and pepper in a blender and process until smooth. Season with salt and pepper to taste.

Makes about 3 cups
(24 fl oz/750 ml); serves 2 or 3

Mint tea slush

Because this recipe calls for a relatively large quantity of frozen tea, you could freeze it in a small, shallow metal or plastic pan rather than in ice cube trays.

2 cups (16 fl oz/500 ml) strong black tea, frozen
1/2 cup (4 fl oz/125 ml) strong tea, chilled
2 tablespoons fresh mint leaves, coarsely chopped
1 tablespoon sugar, or to taste

Allow frozen tea to soften slightly. If tea is one piece rather than ice cubes, break up into smaller pieces. Place frozen tea and remaining ingredients in a blender and process until smooth yet still icy.

Makes about 2 cups
(16 fl oz/500 ml); serves 2

Picture: Spicy Mary

103

glossary of terms

Acidophilus yogurt
Yogurt made with the bacteria culture *Lactobacillus acidophilus*, which is reputed to restore the balance of good bacteria in the intestines.

Anthocyanidin
Flavonoid that forms the blue (or reddish blue) pigment in berries, such as blueberries. See *bioflavonoids*.

Antioxidant
A substance that eliminates free radicals, which are thought to cause cancer. Vitamins can have antioxidant properties (A, C and E are the best known), as can minerals, flavonoids and enzymes.

Beta-carotene
The best known of all the carotenoids, which is converted to vitamin A in the body. Carrots are particularly rich in this mineral.

Bioflavonoids or flavonoids
The colorful pigments in some fruits and vegetables, which is also present in citrus pith and membrane. They have antioxidant properties as well as other health applications.

Buttermilk
Buttermilk is a cultured milk product, slightly thick, and usually quite low in fat. It has a pleasant, tangy flavor.

Carob powder
Finely ground, roasted carob pod. It is similar in appearance, flavor and texture to cocoa powder, and is often used as a substitute. It is nutritious, and caffeine free.

Diuretic
A substance that increases the excretion of urine.

Enzymes
Proteins that act as a catalyst for metabolic functions in the body, such as breaking down foods so the body can absorb the nutrients.

Flaxseed
Also known as linseed. Flaxseed is a good source of omega-3 fatty acids,

which have many health benefits, including the prevention of heart disease.

Free radicals
Incomplete oxygen molecules that attack and oxidize other molecules. Antioxidants work to allay this reaction. The body can tolerate a certain amount of free radical activity, but when it exceeds the capacity of antioxidants present, cell damage can occur.

Lactose
The natural sugar present in milk.

Lassi
A drink from India, usually based on yogurt and ice.

Laxative
A substance that stimulates excretion from the bowel.

Lycopene
A carotenoid present in ripe tomatoes and red papaya, which may help to prevent prostate cancer.

Osteoporosis
A condition affecting bone density. Bones become brittle and may break or fracture easily. Preventative measures include an adequate calcium intake, as well as regular weight bearing exercise.

Protein whey powder
A dairy by-product which is added to drinks as a dietary supplement, to increase protein intake.

Psyllium husks
A gentle soluble fiber which passes easily though the body, helping to alleviate constipation.

Rose water
A flavoring used in Middle Eastern and Indian cuisines. It is said to have cooling and nourishing properties, as well as imparting a slightly floral aroma and flavor.

Tofu
A curd made by adding a setting agent to soy milk. It can be either firm or soft (silken). The soft variety is

required for drink recipes, to give a smooth consistency.

Vegan
A person who does not consume any animal products, as opposed to vegetarians who may consume milk, cheese or eggs, but avoid meat.

Wheat germ
Part of the wheat grain discarded in the processing of white flour. It is very nutritious rich in vitamin E and B vitamins.

Zest
The thin colored part of the skin on citrus fruit (not including the white pith). It contains aromatic oils which give intense flavour. Use fine holes on a grater to lightly grate the zest from the fruit.

ingredients index

A

Almond
    apricot and almond smoothie 30
    fruit and nut smoothie 33
    muesli mix 47
    praline shake 90
Amaretti apricot parfait shake 93
Apple
    apples à la mode 86
    berry and apple smoothie 37
    high-fiber smoothie 22
Apricot
    apricot and almond smoothie 30
    apricot parfait shake 93
    apricot smoothie 41
    breakfast smoothie 34
Apricot nectar and passion fruit shake 51
Avocado
    about 10
    preparing 14
    avocado shots 71
    restorative smoothie 22

B

Banana
    banana and date smoothie 25
    banana and raisin blend 48
    banana blitz 100
    banana split shake 58
    banana–buttermilk blend 29
    blueberry and banana frappe 72
    breakfast smoothie 34
    favorite banana smoothie 29
    fruit salad smoothie 37
    fruit shake 54
    papaya, banana and lime frappe 71
    passion fruit and banana smoothie 38
    pineapple–coconut whip 48
    protein power smoothie 22
    restorative smoothie 22
    tamarillo, banana and kiwifruit frappe 76

    tropical smoothie 33
    warm banana–chocolate float 97
Beet, orange and grape blend 79
Black currant shake 54
Blackberry smoothie 30
Blueberry
    berry yogurt thick-shake 58
    berry–citrus blend 79
    blueberry and banana frappe 72
    blueberry cheesecake shake 86
    purple passion 79
Brazil nut restorative smoothie 22
Buttermilk
    about 105
    buttermilk–banana blend 29
Butterscotch–pecan shake 90

C

Cantaloupe
    about 10
    cantaloupe crush 48
    carrot and cantaloupe blend 80
    red papaya and cantaloupe frappe 76
Caramel
    caramel–date milk shake 61
    chocolate–caramel thick-shake 65
    crème caramel shake 89
    milk shake 57
Carrot and cantaloupe blend 80
Cashew mango oat-milk shake 44
Celery vegetable crush 75
Cherimoya
    about 10
    cherimoya shake 47
Cherry
    Black Forest shake 89
    cherry–berry smoothie 25
    chocolate–cherry–coconut shake 97
Chocolate
    chocolate berry shake 93
    chocolate milk shake 61

    chocolate–cherry–coconut shake 97
    chocolate–orange shake 57
    double-chocolate thick-shake 65
    mocha latte shake 57
    warm banana–chocolate float 97
Chocolate cookie shake 93
Chocolate ice cream
    Black Forest shake 89
    chocolate berry shake 93
    chocolate–caramel thick-shake 65
    coffee thick-shake 103
    double-chocolate thick-shake 65
    mocha latte shake 57
Chocolate, white, warm marshmallow bliss 94
Coconut
    mango and toasted coconut shake 97
    pineapple–coconut whip 48
Coconut milk
    banana blitz 100
    chocolate–cherry–coconut shake 97
    papaya, lime and coconut smoothie 51
    tropical smoothie 33
Coffee
    espresso freeze 89
    iced coffee shake 62
    iced soy latte 47
    mocha latte shake 57
    thick-shake 103
    tiramisu shake 86
Cointreau strawberry daiquiri 100
Coring fruit 17
Cranberry
    cranberry, orange and pineapple frappe 75
    cranberry-vanilla smoothie 33
Cream cheese blueberry cheesecake shake 86
Cucumber avocado shots 71
Custard apple see Cherimoya

D

Dates
    about 13

index

pitting 16
banana and date smoothie 25
caramel–date milk shake 61
tahini–date smoothie 51
Dried apple and apricot muesli mix 47

F
Fig
about 10
fresh fig and ginger smoothie 38
Filbert chocolate berry shake 93
Flaxseed
about 106
flaxseed and pear smoothie 41
Freezing fruit 18
Frozen yogurt berry shake 25

G
Ginger
fresh fig and ginger smoothie 38
mango and ginger lassi 26
mango, peach and ginger frappe 68
smoothie soother 34
Golden raisin
banana and raisin blend 48
fruit and nut smoothie 33
Grape
beet, orange and grape blend 79
watermelon and grape ice 83
Grapefruit, ruby see Ruby grapefruit
Green tea and melon frappe 83

H
Hazelnut chocolate berry shake 93
Honeydew melon
about 11
green tea and melon frappe 83
minty melon mix 68
Honey–macadamia shake 61

I
Ice cream, chocolate see Chocolate ice
cream
Ice cream, soy see Soy ice cream

K
Kiwifruit
about 11
peeling 16
minty melon mix 68
tamarillo, banana and kiwifruit frappe 76

L
Lassi
about 106
mango and ginger lassi 26
pineapple-mint lassi 26
Lemon
avocado shots 71
lemon smoothie 41
lemon–passion fruit shake 54
Lime
papaya, banana and lime frappe 71
papaya, lime and coconut smoothie 51
raspberry, plum and lime frappe 80

M
Macadamia nut
banana and raisin blend 48
honey–macadamia shake 61
Malted milk shake, vanilla 62
Mandarin shake, creamy 94
Mango
about 11
preparing 14
mango and ginger lassi 26
mango and toasted coconut shake 97
mango milk shake 58
mango oat-milk shake 44
mango, peach and ginger frappe 68
mango, pineapple and passion fruit frappe 75
papaya, pineapple and mango frappe 71
peach and mango low-fat smoothie 38
tropical smoothie 33
Maple, pear and pecan smoothie 26
Marshmallow bliss, warm 94
Mascarpone tiramisu shake 86
Melon, cantaloupe see Cantaloupe
Melon, honeydew see Honeydew melon
Morello cherry Black Forest shake 89
Mulberry and apple smoothie 37

N
Nectarine
fruit salad smoothie 37
grapefruit and nectarine frappe 80
O
Oat milk
about 43
mango oat-milk shake 44
muesli mix 47
Orange
beet, orange and grape blend 79
berry–citrus blend 79
blueberry and banana frappe 72
cantaloupe crush 48
carrot and cantaloupe blend 80
chocolate–orange shake 57
cranberry, orange and pineapple frappe 75
fruit salad smoothie 37
orange sherbet shake 62
orange–peach smoothie 44
pineapple, orange and strawberry frappe 68
rhubarb smoothie 94

P
Papaya
about 11
papaya, banana and lime frappe 71
papaya, lime and coconut smoothie 51
papaya, pineapple and mango frappe 71
smoothie soother 34
Papaya, red see Red papaya
Passion fruit
about 12
preparing 15
apricot and passion fruit shake 51
lemon–passion fruit shake 54
mango, pineapple and passion fruit frappe 75
passion fruit and banana smoothie 38
purple passion 79
Peach
cherimoya shake 47
mango, peach and ginger frappe 68
orange–peach smoothie 44
peach and mango low-fat smoothie 38
peaches and cream shake 90

pink peach frappe 72
summertime blend 37
Peanut butter banana split shake 58
Pear
    coring 17
    pear and flaxseed smoothie 41
    pear, pecan and maple smoothie 26
    pomegranate and pear ice 83
Pecan
    butterscotch–pecan shake 90
    pear, pecan and maple smoothie 26
Peeling fruit 15
Peppermint patty shake 65
Persimmon
    about 12
    pineapple–persimmon crush 76
Pineapple
    about 12
    coring 17
    banana blitz 100
    cranberry, orange and pineapple frappe 75
    mango, pineapple and passion fruit frappe 75
    papaya, pineapple and mango frappe 71
    pineapple-mint lassi 26
    pineapple, orange and strawberry frappe 68
    pineapple–coconut whip 48
    pineapple–persimmon crush 76
    purple passion 79
    smoothie soother 34
    tropical smoothie 33
Pistachio smoothie, spiced 34
Pitting fruit 16
Plum
    pink peach frappe 72
    raspberry, plum and lime frappe 80
    spiced plum smoothie 30
Pomegranate
    about 12
    juicing 17
    pomegranate and pear ice 83
Prune high-fiber smoothie 22

R
Raspberry
    berry yogurt thick-shake 58
    berry–citrus blend 79
    chocolate berry shake 93
    raspberry, plum and lime frappe 80
    summertime blend 37
Red bell pepper vegetable crush 75
Red papaya
    about 13
    red papaya and cantaloupe frappe 76
Rhubarb smoothie 94
Rice milk
    about 43
    banana and raisin blend 48
    cherimoya shake 47
Rockmelon see Cantaloupe
Ruby grapefruit
    about 13
    grapefruit and nectarine frappe 80

S
Selecting fruit 18
Sorbet
    about 43
    lemon smoothie 41
    lemon–passion fruit shake 54
    mango and toasted coconut shake 97
    mango milk shake 58
    mango oat-milk shake 44
    peach and mango low-fat smoothie 38
    pineapple–coconut whip 48
Soy ice cream
    about 43
    apricot and passion fruit shake 51
    cherimoya shake 47
    iced soy latte 47
Soy milk
    about 43
    iced soy latte 47
    strawberry–soy thick-shake 44
    tahini–date smoothie 51
Soy yogurt
    cantaloupe crush 48
    muesli mix 47
    orange–peach smoothie 44
Spicy Mary 103
Storing fruit 18
Strawberry
    berry shake 25
    berry–citrus blend 79
    cherry–berry smoothie 25
    fruit salad smoothie 37
    fruit shake 54
    pineapple, orange and strawberry frappe 68
    pink peach frappe 72
    strawberry daiquiri 100
    strawberry smoothie 29
    strawberry–soy thick-shake 44
    watermelon, strawberry and mint frappe 72
Sultana see Golden raisin

T
Tahini–date smoothie 51
Tamarillo
    about 13
    tamarillo, banana and kiwifruit frappe 76
Tea slush, mint 103
Tofu
    about 106
    protein power smoothie 22
    strawberry–soy thick-shake 44
Tomato
    spicy Mary 103
    vegetable crush 75

W
Watermelon
    watermelon and grape ice 83
    watermelon, strawberry and mint frappe 72
White chocolate warm marshmallow bliss 94

Y
Yogurt
    about 21, 105
Yogurt, frozen, berry shakes 25
Yogurt, soy see Soy yogurt

health index

A

Acidophilus 21, 22, 34, 105
Anthocyanidin 105
Antibacterials 75
Antioxidants 13, 30, 41, 44, 76, 79, 80, 83, 105
Antivirals 75
Arteries 79

B

Bacteria, intestinal 34
Beta-carotene 10, 11, 13, 30, 41, 58, 72, 76, 80, 105
Bioflavonoids 75, 79, 105
Blood 21
Bones 21
Bromelain 12, 34, 48

C

Caffeine 57
Calcium 10, 12, 13, 21, 22, 38, 43, 44, 51, 54, 79, 94
Cholesterol 10, 61

D

Degeneration 79
Dietary fiber 10, 13, 30, 34, 38, 48, 80
Digestion 11, 12, 34, 48, 68, 72
Disease prevention 79
Diuretics 75, 105

E

Enzymes 11, 12, 34, 48, 106
Eyesight 79

F

Fat, unsaturated 10, 22, 30, 34, 44, 51, 61
Fiber, dietary 10, 13, 30, 34, 38, 48, 80
Fber, soluble 22
Flavonoids 75, 79, 105

Folic acid 79
Free radicals 80, 106

G

Gout 25
Growth 22

H

Heart disease 22, 41, 44
Heart muscle 71
Hormone production 22

I

Immune system 71
Intestinal bacteria 34
Iron 10, 12, 13, 22, 33, 79

L

Lactobacillus acidophilus 21, 22, 34, 105
Lactose 43
Laxatives 22, 106
Lycopene 13, 75, 76, 106

M

Magnesium 13, 34, 44, 62
Menopause 21
Monounsaturated fat 22, 34
Morning sickness 68
Motion sickness 68
Muscle function 21

N

Nausea 68

O

Omega-3 fatty acids 41
Osteoporosis 21, 106

P

Papain 11, 34

Pectin 22
Phosphorus 62
Potassium 10, 11, 12, 13, 22, 25, 33, 34, 47, 71, 75, 76, 79, 94
Pregnancy 21
Prostate cancer 75
Protein 22, 44

S

Selenium 22
Sodium 71
Soluble fiber 22
Stomach 34

T

Teeth 21
Thiamine 12, 34, 94

U

Unsaturated fat 10, 22, 30, 34, 44, 51, 61
Urinary-tract infections 33

V

Veins 79
Vitamin A 10, 12, 13, 38, 44, 54
Vitamin B 10, 47
Vitamin B1 44
Vitamin B2 44
Vitamin B6 34
Vitamin C 10, 11, 12, 13, 30, 33, 38, 44, 47, 48, 51, 54, 58, 75, 76, 79, 80
Vitamin D 33
Vitamin E 11, 22, 30, 47

W

Weight gain 22

guide to weights and measures

The conversions given in the recipes in this book are approximate. Whichever system you use, remember to follow it consistently, thereby ensuring that the proportions are consistent throughout a recipe.

WEIGHTS

Imperial	Metric
$1/3$ oz	10 g
$1/2$ oz	15 g
$3/4$ oz	20 g
1 oz	30 g
2 oz	60 g
3 oz	90 g
4 oz ($1/4$ lb)	125 g
5 oz ($1/3$ lb)	150 g
6 oz	180 g
7 oz	220 g
8 oz ($1/2$ lb)	250 g
9 oz	280 g
10 oz	300 g
11 oz	330 g
12 oz ($3/4$ lb)	375 g
16 oz (1 lb)	500 g
2 lb	1 kg
3 lb	1.5 kg
4 lb	2 kg

VOLUME

Imperial	Metric	Cup
1 fl oz	30 ml	
2 fl oz	60 ml	$1/4$
3 fl oz	90 ml	$1/3$
4 fl oz	125 ml	$1/2$
5 fl oz	150 ml	$2/3$
6 fl oz	180 ml	$3/4$
8 fl oz	250 ml	1
10 fl oz	300 ml	$1^{1}/4$
12 fl oz	375 ml	$1^{1}/2$
13 fl oz	400 ml	$1^{2}/3$
14 fl oz	440 ml	$1^{3}/4$
16 fl oz	500 ml	2
24 fl oz	750 ml	3
32 fl oz	1 L	4

USEFUL CONVERSIONS

$1/4$ teaspoon	1.25 ml
$1/2$ teaspoon	2.5 ml
1 teaspoon	5 ml
1 Australian tablespoon	20 ml (4 teaspoons)
1 UK/US tablespoon	15 ml (3 teaspoons)

First published in Great Britain in 2003 by Aurum Press Ltd
25 Bedford Avenue, London WC1B 3AT

First published by Lansdowne Publishing Pty Ltd, 2003
Level 1, 18 Argyle St, Sydney NSW 2000, Australia

Commissioned by Deborah Nixon
Text: Tracy Rutherford
Photography and styling: Vicki Liley
Photography pp 10–19: Joe Filshie
Designer: Grant Slaney, The Modern Art Production Group
Cover Design: Bettina Hodgson
Editor: Judith Dunham
Production Manager: Sally Stokes
Project Coordinator: Bettina Hodgson
Props: liley & liley

A catalogue reference is available from the British Library.

ISBN 1 85410 888 3

10 9 8 7 6 5 4 3 2 1
2007 2006 2005 2004 2003

Set in Helvetica on QuarkXPress
Printed in Singapore